The Yellow Creek Story

By

L.M. 'Yellow Creek' Watson

As Told To A.D. Holcombe

Revised Edition

Original Cover by Iris Reynolds
Wadesville, Indiana

A.D. Holcombe original copyrighted 1954

© **2021 Emmanuel Books, LLC.**

All rights reserved. No part of this publication may be reproduced, stored in a retrieval system or transmitted in any form or by any means, electronic, mechanical, photocopying, recording or otherwise without the prior permission of the publisher or in accordance with the provisions of the Copyright, Designs and Patents Act 1988 or under the terms of any license permitting limited copying issued by the Copyright Licensing Agency.

Originally Published by Tri-State Printers, Inc. Bucklin, Missouri 1954 A.D. Holcombe

Published by:
Emmanuel Books, LLC.
Edwards, MO, USA

Typesetting: Cambria

Cover Design: Original Cover Design by Iris Reynolds

This revised edition is for the sole purposes of The Yellow Creek Story distribution and honoring L.M. "Yellow Creek Watson" and the works of A.D. Holcombe. All credits given to L.M Watson and A.D. Holcombe. Formatting and page numbers may differ from the original text.

ISBN-978-1-7331211-7-0 (PB)

Printed in the United States of America

DEDICATION

This book is respectfully dedicated by the writer-publisher to L.M. (Yellow Creek) Watson; whose life work with hounds of all kinds has been of quality of which this nation's breeders of dogs may justly be proud; and whose forthright courage in standing behind his convictions has made this book possible. Within these pages will be found information and ideas developed over many years of observation and study of hundreds of hounds, which resulted in the strain of hounds known as "The Yellow Creeks." There have never been any better ones of overall quality ever bred anywhere.

FOREWORD

This book was written in the early summer of 1954 for the purpose of placing in print; for those among the present generation, and generations to come, who thrill to the running of hounds; the experiences and conclusions of one of the greatest hound men of them all, L. M. (Yellow Creek) Watson.

"Yeller Creek," as he is known in hunting circles the country over, is one of these few men who possess the keen analytical intelligence and intuition required to successfully breed excellent hounds. Though virtually uneducated formally, his monumental work in developing the famous Yellow Creek strain of hounds stand as testimony to his unexcelled ability.

The blood of the Yellow Creeks of old still today flows through more than 85 percent of all field trial winners and top producing beagles in this country. This works presumes to time capsule in essence the knowledge gained in his lifetime; to the best of the ability to the writer.

                                                              A.D. Holcombe

L.M. "Yellow Creek" Watson

TABLE OF CONTENTS

General History..1

History – Beagles...14

Hunting Quality...37

Conformity...44

Training...55

Field Trials...59

Breeding...73

ILLUSTRATIONS

Pat, brother to Hasty...................................11

Yellow Creek Ty Cobb................................18

Wheatley's Chieftan....................................36

Yellow Creek Mme.
And Yellow Creek Babbs............................43

Yellow Creek Sport......................................47

Yellow Creek Lucky.....................................54

Yellow Creek Sparky...................................72

THE YELLOW CREEK STORY
By L.M. (Yellow Creek) Watson
(As Told to A.D. Holcombe)

CHAPTER I
Part I
General History

I was born on a farm a few miles from New Boston, Missouri in 1887. The youngest of four children, I was considered by my family to be the "bashfulest kid that ever lived," and my head was covered with a mop of fire-red hair that adequately fit the temper my somewhat Irish descent had stored within me.

In the 1800's if you lived on a farm in Missouri it was most likely that you had close contact with hounds of one sort or another. My father never was too much for them, though his father before him loved them dearly, and my mother's side of the family would not think of being without a few fox or coon hounds around the place. But during my early childhood we had no hounds at all on the farm.

I will never forget the first time I saw a pair of hounds trailing game. I was perhaps six or seven years old at the time, and mother, needing some sour milk to bake bread, had handed me a milk pail and instructed me to hike down the road a few miles to grandmother's farm and get some. It was about eight or nine o'clock on a sunny morning, and as I strolled along I heard the magic sound of dogs barking ahead. With childish curiosity, I investigated and came upon a pair of big hounds running near the road with their noses to the ground. A tall fellow stood nearby along the road, and I watched along with him, mouth open in astonishment, as they worked their way carefully through some open timber, occasionally throwing their heads back and letting go with a tremendous, booming howl.

Yellow Creek Sport

"CH. YELLOW CREEK SPORT"
(Fd. Ch. Yellow Creek Bob x Fd. Ch. Yellow Creek Jessica)

One of the greatest running and producing beagles ever bed in this country. His head and conformity are considered the best possible by L. M. (Yellow Creek) Watson.

They were named Blue Buck and Belle, and were blue ticked all over their slender bodies. I was so fascinated with them that I quickly forgot all thoughts of the sour milk, and followed them as fast as I could leg it. I chased them until they denned and a rabbit, and then I poked it out with a stick and they caught it and ate it, and I thought it was the darnedest, most interesting thing I ever saw in my whole life! And so the day went. I poked out several rabbits for the big hounds, and most of the time they would catch them quickly and eat them just as quickly. From then on it was just hounds for me.

As the poet says, suddenly the day was far spent, and I began to realize with some disquieting feelings that I had not accomplished my errand. It was quite late in the evening when I returned home, and mother had a lot to say about where I had been all day, but when I explained to her what had happened she didn't whip me. Years later, I learned that it was because on her side of the family men folk had often tarried to the sound of hounds, and she was quite adjusted to the procedure. I don't think I ever knew of a woman who liked to hear hounds run as much as she did.

We moved to another farm when I was ten years old, and that spring of 97 I got my first hound. It was a sort of black and tan by nature, but was nearly half white. Jeff Davis Nester, a neighbor of ours and a great hound man, gave it to me in appreciation for my avid interest in hounds. I lived about every joyful moment from then on with that hound. We chased foxes, coons and wolves at night, and rabbits by day. He was a good hound by any standard. One day he went with a pack of six neighbor's hounds on a wolf chase that ended up 60 miles away when they put the big fellow at bay and killed him. A farmer who lived near the spot where the wolf was destroyed, fed the hounds, rested them in his corn crib overnight, and turned them loose the next morning. They all returned that night, and you can't imagine how proud I was that my hound stayed right in there to the end.

A short while later he and two other hounds chased a wolf out of the country. They were seen running about ten miles away, headed Southwest. Two of the hounds returned a few days later, but mine never did come back. I owned no more hounds until after I was married in 1907, but the fever burned within me, and I frequently went on fox and coon chases with neighbors.

During this period, my brother was interested in hounds and he had quite a number of them. Two of them, a mother and her son, were two of the best big hounds I ever knew of, and therein lies a story or two, since they were related to the great Tennessee Lead through Petit's Bone.

My grandfather was born in Ohio, and migrated to the town of Salesburg (as I recall it being spelled) Kentucky, to begin the trade of saddlemaker. The rangy Cumberland Mountains separated Kentucky from Tennessee, and Salesburg is not far from this rugged area. Probably this part of America is endowed with some of the greatest foxhound men who ever lived, and the hounds they developed have become the backbone of most of our hounds today. "Wash" Mauphin was a wealthy landowner who kept two running packs of top-notch foxhounds, about 16 in a pack. The famous Walker brothers also lived near there, and Mauphin and the Walker brothers often ran hounds together in the Cumberland mountains, on the Tennessee side, for weeks at a time in order to determine which were the best ones, and which ones to breed. They made this trip frequently because there were red foxes to be found there, whereas Kentucky had only gray foxes at that time.

Mauphin, in addition to having the best hounds he could get his hands on, also had the best riding horses. They were called "Copperbottoms"-- most of them were roans, built on the racehorse order -- and he rode to the dogs and hollered at them in a tremendous, booming voice whenever the race was hot and the mood suited him.

Grandfather, as Mauphin's saddlemaker, came to know him well, and it was through his friendship that I subsequently heard the story of the finding of Tennessee

Lead. On several successive trips to the Cumberland Mountains, Mauphin and the Walker brothers heard a strange voice in their packs. Occasionally they got a look at the stray hound that was joining in, and each time he was giving their own hounds a severe drubbing. The exceptional quality of this hound excited Mauphin to no end, and he determined to buy him regardless of cost. He sent some of his men inquiring in the area, but could find no one who knew of the strange big hound. At length an old woman who lived alone in a small cabin shed some light on the mystery when she explained that a strange dog had come to her house "some months ago", emancipated and hungry. She had fed the big hound intermittently for some time, but had never been able to get near enough to him to touch him. She indicated that she felt no one owned the hound and that it would be all right with her if he was taken so he could be fed regularly.

Upon hearing this, Mauphin ordered a large, strong pen to be built near where the hound was usually fed, with the entrance left open. He left feed for the hound, and instructed the woman to leave it inside the pen. The hound turned up one evening, and after much suspicion he entered the pen and ate. On Mauphin's next trip he had a specially built spring door with him, which he had fitted to the entrance, and shortly thereafter the hound was caught.

He was a big hound, and powerfully built, and it was not without considerable difficulty that he was transferred into a portable cage and taken back to Mauphin's kennels for taming and training. Mauphin had a negro hound trainer who was considered to be the best in the country. He could bring out the best of any hound, and it took him nearly a year to train the hound to handle. The hound was named Tennessee Lead for obvious reasons. He was seal brown in color, with some white on him.

Lead was used at stud extensively by both Mauphin and the Walker brothers, and everyone in the area as well. He was a great sire, and probably one of the greatest in forming the backbone of today's good hound strains.

Many stories were told of Tennessee Lead. The one that my grandfather told that intrigued me most was about the time Lead fell into a sinkhole in the Cumberland Mountains. He was this day, as usual, leading the pack by some distance when he fell headlong into a deep, black hole. Sinkholes as grandfather described them were of varying depths, and there were three main hazards involved in them. First, the bottoms were usually soft and mucky, and if the fall didn't kill a hound, the bottom might suck him in. Second, the bottoms were considered to be good places to find copperhead snakes in large numbers, and third, a gas called "damp" was found in many of them which could replace oxygen and snuff out the life of any living thing that fell in the hole. This damp, it was said, would put out a flame if ignited.

Lead, said grandfather, had fallen into a hole of considerable depth, and Mauphin was fit to be tied. Observers could hear Lead at the bottom, so knew he had survived the fall, and the damp. About everyone gave Lead up for lost except Mauphin. He went around the neighborhood towns and offered a reward of one dollar per foot to anyone who would be lowered into the hole to rescue the big hound. At length a daredevil of a young fellow agreed to do it, and a brand new winch was bought and installed over the sinkhole. The young fellow was lowered slowly into the hole with a new rope secured around his waist. He carried with him another rope with instructions that if he changed his mind part way down he was to tug on it a prearranged signal, and he would be brought up immediately no questions asked. If he went to the bottom and found Lead, he was to tie a hitch around the hounds chest behind the four legs and signal for him to be brought up.

Slowly the young fellow was lowered into the sinkhole, and he went down nearly 65 feet before he was able to reach down and touch Lead. He then quickly tied a hitch around the hound, and they both were brought to the surface to the cheers of onlookers.

A few years after this incident, grandfather left for Indiana where he married my grandmother. Together they came across the Wabash River, down the Mississippi, and finally on horse to Missouri with their possessions. Grandfather brought a few hounds with him, but I never learned what became of them.

Sometime later the covered wagon caravans began to move west, and every now and then a family in one of them would look over our section of the country and decide they had gone far enough. They settled down and built cabins along the streams in order to ensure enough water supply, and as more and more of them came and settled down, a pattern emerged. The people who lived along a certain creek picked up its name in general terms. Those who lived along Dry Creek, for instance, might have a reputation for being good builders, or superior farmers, and they would be referred to as "the Dry Creekers." My family settled along Yellow Creek, which was noted for harboring tough, sinewy farmers. They were called, of course, the Yellow Creekers, and at the occasional celebrations and dances that were held in those days where drinking was heavy and fighting not the least of the fun, the Yellow Creekers always more than held their own. They had courage aplenty, and never knew quit, irrespective of odds. Years later when I began to cast around for a name for my kennels, I didn't have far to look. As far as I can determine, the Yellow Creek Kennels were the first ever named for a stream, or such location.

In these days, Indians still roamed the countryside, and buffalo were in large numbers. Keeping alive was somewhat a chore, and at times required considerable ingenious. Still, the covered wagons were rolled West. Before I was born the Petit family came through, and stopped off in our country. Petit had come from Mauphin's hometown in Kentucky, and had brought with him some excellent hounds that actually started this sections hound stock by their exceptional quality. They stood out far above everything my grandfather had seen in this area. One of his bitches was close to Lead, and bread into that strain while Petit was in Kentucky. In the resulting litter, born enroute, or soon after Petit's arrival here, was a hound later named Petit's Bone. This hound carried a tremendous reputation in this part of Missouri when I was a youngster, and my brother managed to acquire some young stock from this breeding, three or four generations after Bone.

They were all good hounds, and reproduced well. Some of them were exceptional and above what anyone would expect of a hound. We rarely ever went outside of our area to get hounds for this reason, a pattern which later colored my breeding ideas to a considerable extent.

One of my brother's males was named Danny Pro- -We called him Jeff--and when bred to Cora, an especially good bitch, a litter of 9 puppies resulted. They were black, white and tan, and among them was a small female that stood out from the day they were born. She was keen, level-headed, and quick as you ever saw. At that time there was an exceptional little filly named Hasty running the County Fair circuits and cleaning up everything in sight, so naturally we named this hound Hasty.

At six months of age you could hold Hasty up above your head and no matter what attitude you held her in, you could drop her and she would without fail land on her feet like a cat. She matured at about 21 inches in height, and was slim. She always retained her uncanny sense of balance, and when she was driving a fox she would slide through fences sideways like a fish, never losing a step, and land on her feet in such a way as to continue her running motion perfectly. Born in June, she saw her first fox the following February. I had her out for a walk, and she met the fox head-on in a forest. The fox was at the time being chased by some hounds, and being somewhat distracted from behind, he did not see Hasty until he had nearly run into her. Hasty became a foxhound from that moment, and she ran all night on that fox. Next morning when I got up she was in the barn still wringing wet.

Her exceptional quality never dimmed. Before she was a year old she was a tough one to beat, and in April-- before she was yet a year old-- she demonstrated to me that she was a hound among hounds. We were hunting foxes with a pack, and came across a track. Every hound but Hasty went unhesitatingly Northeast on it, and when she cut out in the opposite direction I alone began to doubt her wisdom. However, the others ran about a mile and then came back looking kind of foolish and started out after Hasty. By the time they got back to us, and followed Hasty and her fox, the trail was too cold for the conditions and they were unable to keep to the trail for long. Hasty came back the next day after running all night. She had an exceptional nose, and never made a wrong bark that I knew of. She was one of those good ones you don't often find, and I determined to get some of her blood to initiate my own kennels.

Our usual practice in fox hunting was to hitch up the buggy and start out for an area about twelve miles away where the foxes weren't so scarce. The hounds would string out loosely behind the buggy, and after we got there, they would go to work and find game. The second time Hasty went with us to this area, she realized where we were going and by the time we arrived with the rest of the hounds we found her there, already running a fox!

It was on this day that I saw her do something I've rarely seen a hound do since, with the exception of watching her brother Pat do it consistently. We had about 21 hounds in the pack, made up of some of the neighbor's good ones, and including five hounds owned by a fellow named Brown. One of these five was a son of Fd. Ch. Scrape, the Kentucky hound, and the other four were all good ones. When the hounds were all in pack and running nicely, we took a seat near the top of a ridge and sat down to wait for some action. After about two hours of running we could hear the pack swinging directly up the ridge toward us, and about this time we heard another fox barking ahead of them some distance up the ridge. We assumed correctly that this fox was planning to "change off" with the fox being run, and he continued to bark intermittently until the pack was quite close. Apparently he ran straight ahead up the ridge, and the fox being run cut off at right angles and went over into the valley. As the pack came past us, Hasty was leading, but when they reached the approximate spot where we had heard the new fox barking, her tongue went quiet. The rest of the pack, taking the new fox's trail, went on up the ridge with booming voices, and it was only a few minutes time when we heard Hasty running at right angles to the ridge into the valley, on the trail of the original fox! She continued to run her fox for some time, when finally the two foxes came together, bringing Hasty and the pack together. This occurred within hearing of us, and presently there were two packs running, Hasty leading a small one. Later when this small pack came past us we saw that it consisted of four hounds that had hearkened to Hasty, and the remainder of the pack held to their fox. At first, I was somewhat reluctant to believe this demonstration of nose and level-headedness, in the light of my previous experiences, but after she repeated the performance several times I realized it was so. Hasty would never let foxes switch on her from that moment. They tell me beagles will do the same on rabbits, but in all my experiences with hundreds of them I never saw this happen in a way that I could conclusively prove it.

    Hasty was not for sale, so I bought her brother Pat. He had been sold as a puppy, and after seeing Hasty I looked him up and bought him from his owner, George Thomas. George later told me he ran Pat on seven successive nights on foxes with different packmates, and Pat ran solidly with the best, doing more than his share. He proved as good at coon hunting as he was a foxhound. After this time I owned and bred literally thousands of fox and coon hounds, and shipped them to all parts of the country. They had a great deal of Tennessee Lead through Petit's Bone in them at first, but after a while the

blood got thinned out by the use of outside hounds and they became my own idea of good hounds.

As for breeding theories, I bred them the same way I would breed beagles. About the only general way I feel about breeding them is, "breed the best to the best." Since the breeding ideas are the same, the chapter on breeding beagles will tell the story. The one chief characteristic of all my hounds has been <u>level-headedness with the courage to back it up</u>. A hound without this all-important factor is no hound at all. There are, of course, many other requirements that go to make up a good hound, but I consider level-headedness and courage far and away the most important.

A few years ago I owned a pair of hounds that had typical Yellow Creek courage. One was a big fellow about 24 inches high, and the other a hound of perhaps 19 or 20 inches. One fall day we were hunting for a fox trail when the two hounds struck a wolf track and took off out of hearing. At the time I did not know what happened, but guessed. The hounds were gone for three days and nights, and when they turned up the morning of the fourth day they were cut up badly, and their feet worn nearly through the pads. They indicated plenty of aches and bruises, and I told my neighbors that they must have had an awful time with something or other.

The following spring I was visiting a nearby town when a fellow from Harris, Mo about 65 miles from New Boston, joined in the conversation and asked if I was L. M. Watson. Learning that I was, he told me he had put off writing to me, and recited the following story. The previous fall some hounds had been heard running in the vicinity of his farm during the entire night, and the following day they began to bark "treed" in a spot in the woods near the farm next to his. At that farm lived a boy of about fourteen years who, upon hearing he barking in one place for several hours, decided to investigate. He took with him a walking stick and his two dogs, a small part-hound, and a large shepherd dog that greatly enjoyed fighting with every dog in the neighborhood.

After a brisk hike he came up on the scene and found two hounds trying to get at a wolf that was at bay underneath a ledge of rocks. The wolf was situated quite well with his body out of sight, and only one dog at a time could get at him, with the result that he was doing a job on the dogs with his teeth. The attackers were definitely at a disadvantage, and the situation was not helped by the arrival of the boy, since the shepherd dog immediately attacked one of the two hounds. When the hound turned to fight with its attacker, the other hound also turned his attention to the new fray. In this brief interim the wolf sensed that it was as good a time as any to depart in some haste, and he sneaked from beneath the rocks and started to slip away. However, the smaller hound had not concentrated so thoroughly on the shepherd dog but that he was still paying attention to the denned wolf, and he quickly turned and nailed the escaping wolf by the hind leg. This brought about a genuine melee of the riot quality, which scared the youngster out of his wits. It finally ended with the wolf dead, and the shepherd dog fleeing for home. The boy salvaged enough of the wolf to claim the bounty, and noticed that the head of the wolf contained only one tusk, and that one was considerably blunted, which had put him to a severe disadvantage, though his size and ruggedness enabled him to keep the hounds at bay while the ledge of rocks gave him adequate protection.

The youngster tried to take the two hounds home with him to feed them, but only the smaller one would come to him. On the collar of this one he read my name and address, and as he led the hound home, the larger hound followed along in the adjoining field. He fed the one hound and left food out for the other. Next day he left the smaller one loose, the other joined it almost immediately from the field nearby, and the pair took off to the Southwest.

Hounds with that kind of hunting instincts are the ones I've always liked to see and have tried to breed. You don't get them too often, but when you do get them it was worth the effort.

One of the biggest headaches I've had in shipping fox and coon hounds to people is that it is impossible to know what their standards for a good hound are, and also whether the conditions under which they will be run are at all like the ones on which they have been trained. Sometimes it takes a hound some time to become accustomed to new smells in new climates and situations. Many times I've shipped a hound that I knew was a good one to two or three owners, who shipped him back indicating they were dissatisfied, and the next man I shipped him to would write me that it was one of the best he ever saw.

To my judgment, fox and coon hounds today are every bit as good as they were during my lifetime, and there seems to be less variation in them than in beagles for quality. As in breeding beagles, I strived to establish a strain of hounds that would reproduce mostly all good hounds and I succeeded in doing so by using the same breeding ideas.

PART II
History
Beagles

To the best of my recollection, it was in 1909 that I saw my first beagle. I had subscribed for some time to a magazine then known as Fox & Hound, which a few years later came to be known as Hounds & Hunting. I had read considerable about beagles, but had never come across one. Fred O'Flyng was editor at the time, and he published quite a bit of material about beagles that I found interesting. Among the ads in one issue I saw one placed by Harry Stroh, of Oregon, Illinois, advertising for a trainer for some of his Ganymede derbies.

I wrote to Stroh and told him that I knew nothing about beagles in particular, but considerable about hounds in general, and that I had plenty of time and game to work them on. Presently I received a phone call from him, and he told me that he liked the fee I charged, and that since I was situated right on a direct rail line from him to me he would ship me two for training, even though he had never heard of me. Shortly thereafter the two hounds arrived, and they turned out to be Ganymede (Davey) Crockett, and Ganymede Chirrup. Sired by Driver, an English hound, they were from a couple of his good Ganymede bitches.

I liked beagles right from the start, and these two were of good quality--especially Davey. I kept this pair for six months, gave them plenty of work, and then shipped them back to Stroh, who was very well pleased with them. In fact, the following year he sent me several to train, and his recommendation brought me many others for training. Soon I had all I could handle and by 1911 and 1912 I had quite a string around the place.

At the time I bought my first three beagles. I purchased Yellow Creek Daisy (Rader's Daniel x Ganymede Cherry) from Stroh; Elora's Blue Peach (The Bat x Elora Blue Juniata) from Dr. C. W. Sanford, Arlington Hgts., Illinois, who had imported her from Hiram Card of Canada;

and Lucille Love (Sir Florist x Jack's Mollie) from Willett Randall, North Creek, N.Y.

Doc Sanford owned the Muskeag Kennels, and he had a lot of good hounds. Afton's Uncle Sam was getting "hot" at about this time, and Doc Sanford began to go overboard for him. He bred a bitch he called Muskeag Vic to Uncle Sam and shipped her to me to raise the litter. On the 4th of the following January she whelped a litter of 8, and I raised and trained them, and had my pick of the litter. They turned out to be not worth killing. The bitch I kept I sold to a fellow in Iowa and she ran fairly well, and had a few pretty good puppies, but that was the most of it. All of these puppies were quite like the descriptions I had of Uncle Sam--mouthy and fighters. Every one of his "get" that ever came to my kennels and there were a number of them, all displayed virtually the same characteristics. They would rather fight than run rabbits, and I recall hearing from good sources that in one trial Uncle Sam stopped in the middle of a race to fight with his bracemate. How true these stories are is sometimes hard to say, but judging from his offspring I would say that there could well be credence to the story.

Since I never cared for hounds of any kind that are overly mouthy or that go out of their way to fight, I didn't think much of Uncle Sam, or any of his offspring when it came to matings. It was about 1916 that I was trying to make up my mind about which studs to use on my 3 bitches. J. V. Burton, of the Rock City Beagles, C. W. Sandford, and Harry Stroh all advised me strongly to "use Uncle Sam while he is available" or to use Rock City Sam, a son of Uncle Sam.

A fellow named Otto Gahrling, who was a good friend of Doc Sanford, lived in Arlington Heights, Ill. near Sanford, and he owned an oversized male sired by Sanford's "Davey" Crockett, the hound I had trained out of an excellent bitch, Maywood Queen. Otto wrote to me that in spite of the fact that he owned a butcher shop and could keep his hounds inexpensively, he would rather have his hound out on the farm where he could run and keep in good shape, and he asked me if I would consider keeping him through the spring and summer. I accepted the hound, and it turned out to be Muskeag Sportsman. After he came to my farm and worked with my beagles a while I came to think a great deal of him. He was about 15 1/2 inches, but he had everything just the way I like it in hounds. His voice was deep and resonant, he hunted well, ran a near perfect rabbit, barked "treed" whenever he holed the rabbit, ran all day if allowed to, and above all, he had plenty of brains. He never got over anxious, but used his head in every situation. I soon realized that he was the best I had ever seen up to this time, and later I realized he was about as good as any I ever did see.

When Doc Sanford learned that I was considering using Muskeag Sportsman on my bitches, he was most discouraged with me. Burton said if I would ship one to him he would breed her to Rock City Sam for no cost, in order to prevent me from making a mistake I would long regret.

As every real breeder must do, I did a lot of weighing the evidence. All I had seen of Uncle Sam's stuff didn't suit me at all. All I had seen of Muskeag Sportsman, I liked very well, in the light of my previous experiences with all kinds of hounds. Sportsman was oversized a bit, true, but on the other hand my three bitches were small. After thinking about it at length, I decided to make the mating, and once I made up my mind I went all the way and bred all three of my bitches to him.

I wrote to Otto Gahrling and he gave his consent, and the matings were made. Regardless of whether it was good fortune or good management, those matings produced excellent results. Each of the three litters had six puppies, and in each litter of six, three were males and three were females.

Taking one at a time, they were as follows: The litter by Lucille Love were all good ones not a common hound in the lot. Lucille Love was an excellent hunter, with a big, long, loud voice--one of the loudest I ever heard on a bitch. She was medium speed, true, honest, a real stayer, and had a good level head on her. Like Muskeag Sportsman, she was a true and intelligent companion as well as being good quality in the field. For instance, she learned without being taught to guard anything I left behind with her. Once I left my coat lying on the ground inadvertently, and when a neighbor went by she bared her teeth whenever he ventured too close. When some cows strayed near, she stood her ground and wouldn't let them near it. I got just one litter from her by Muskeag Sportsman, as she died when the litter was 6 weeks old after being over-heated, and drinking too much ice cold water.

Yellow Creek Ty Cobb

"YELLOW CREEK TY COBB"

(Muskeag Sportsman x Lucille Love)

In the litter was Fd. Ch. Concord Dan, one of the key hounds in the Concord stock of hounds later on. He was never defeated at a field trial while running for first place. Yellow Creek Ty Cobb was another male of the litter. He was definitely field champion quality, and had all the intelligence of his sire and dam. He had the trait of guarding things left with him like his mother, and followed me everywhere. The only beagles I ever kept kenneled were bitches in heat, but few hounds ever tried to follow me to visit neighbors, or other such places. Ty Cobb would follow along and sleep on, or under, a neighbor's porch until I came out, no matter what the hour or the temperature. He also learned to go on coon hunts, which I never permitted my beagles to do. When I took out my coon hounds at night, it was an automatic signal for the beagles to stay put wherever they were. But one night Ty Cobb followed me along the trail, out of my sight, and when the big hounds jumped a coon he came past me whining and indicating his desire to go along with the big hounds. It took me so by surprise that he had patiently followed me, and he was such a friend, that I let him go. After that he always repeated the formula, never going into the pack unless I gave him the go-ahead, and he loved it. He got to be an awful good coon hound, and would pitch right in with hounds that were 3 or 4 times his size and do his share, and sometimes a little more. I later sold him to Ike Carrel, and he was subsequently lost to distemper while being professionally handled at a Canadian field trial. Before his loss, however, he sired F.d Ch. Shady Shores Swallow.

The third male in the litter was Yellow Creek Baldy, a 13 1/2 inch male. He had all the field qualities of the others, and was sold to a fellow who gunned over him. As far as I know he never got into a field trial, as was the case of one of the three bitches in the litter. Another of the three bitches was Fye's Beauty. She was a fine, outstanding hound of top quality, and I sold her to a beagler in Pennsylvania. In her first year of competition she had two licensed wins. Still lacking one win that year, she got a 4-

pronged briar in her lungs one day while hunting. Several successive veterinarians were unable to diagnose the difficulty, and after she died the thorn was found. She was such a top-notcher that she won 4th in a licensed trial while she was carrying the thorn that eventually killed her, in her lung!

Yellow Creek Wardie was the other bitch, and I sold her to C. T. Hartman, owner of Concord Kennels. She was a solid part of the foundation stock of the Concorde Kennels of old. Later on Wardie, bred to Yellow Creek Dan, produced Concord Dot, the maternal granddam of Concord Danny Boy and Fd. Ch. Concord Trueboy.

By my standards, that was quite a litter, but no better than the others. The next litter was by Muskeag Sportsman, out of Elora's Blue Peach. She was strictly an English bred hound, and like the other bitch, in no way related to Muskeag Sportsman. Her litter produced Yellow Creek Bob, one of the best hounds I ever owned, and later on I picked him to succeed Muskeag Sportsman in carrying on the line. Bob was extremely rugged in build, and ran a perfect rabbit, at least as near as I ever saw one run. Bob stood out in his litter for overall level-headedness, and I liked him right from the start. However, as is the way sometimes, I needed money and let him go to Martin Anderson, in Norway, Michigan. After he was gone about a year, I realized I had made a bad mistake, and needed him for a stud hound. In a trade I had picked up a hound named Afton's Dancer. He was by Stoke's Place Sapper; an English hound that was a sorry one; and I didn't think too much of Afton's Dancer, either. I ran him for a while with my hounds, and then bread him to one bitch that was too closely bread to my studs. The litter was every one too mouthy for field hounds, but good for show stock. I sold them all to a show man in St Louis, and still had Dancer. I picked out a nice young hound of good quality by Wheatley's Chieftain; a sire I also owned at the time; and together with Afton's Dancer and some cash I made a deal with Anderson for Bob. After I had him back on my farm, I used him as stud as much as I possibly could without getting my "wires crossed" with too-close matings, and then I again sold him for a price so good I couldn't refuse it. With me he never attended a field trial, but when sold later on he finished his field championship readily.

Blue Cap Revival also came out of this litter, and I don't have to tell you much about him. He was a real topnotcher, and was sold to B. F. Zimmer, Gloversville, N. Y., to whom I sold many hounds. Revival was used heavily as stud considering his time, and produced many good hounds. Elora's Blue Dispatch also came from this litter, and again, not much need to be said about him. He ran as well as any in the field, and was an all-round good hound.

In considering these three males, an interesting aspect of breeding comes into play. I will go further in the chapter on breeding. These three hounds often ran together, and if we were to be able to take them out today for an all-day hunt I'm sure when it was over no one could pick one as being better than the other two--that's the kind of hounds they were. Yet, though I had a selection of all three of these sires, I picked Yellow Creek Bob to carry on Muskeag Sportsman's line of hounds, and sold the other two. Today, Bob's name will be found in many more top hounds than either Dispatch or Revival, though Bob was not used nearly so much as the other two. The question in such a case is, how can you tell in advance which one of a given number of good ones will reproduce? For now we'll just leave it that in spite of what those three hounds; Bob, Revival and Dispatch; did in the field, there were qualities about Bob that stood out, made him a better, stronger bet to reproduce than either of his two brothers.

The three bitches in this litter were all good ones, and under 13 inches. I sold them in a lot to Zimmer, and never heard of them again, as is more inclined to happen with bitches than with males.

The third bitch bred to Muskeag Sportsman was Yellow Creek Daisy. The litter was made up of all good hounds, but I kept only one, a male I named Yellow Creek Mike. All the rest were sold to B. F. Zimmer in a single lot.

Sometime later I sold Mike to M. F. Haley, Wilmington, Del., for an excellent price.

The results from these three matings put me in the beagle business in a hurry. Looking back, I attributed the start of my successful Yellow Creeks to that one decision to use Muskeag Sportsman as stud rather than any of the popular studs at that time. I did later on ship Yellow Creek Daisy to J. V. Burton to have him handle her at the Bass Lake, Indiana, field trial. She came in heat while there, so I consented to having her bread to Rock City Sam since he offered to stud him for free, and since everyone thought so much of his offspring. Daisy presently whelped three pups, two bitches and a dog, all of which were as much like the rest of Uncle Sam's get as you would ever want to see. They were flashy and fast, but mouthy and would rather fight than eat anytime.

Then and there I made a decision that I never wavered from, no matter how tempting it seemed therafter -- I never again bred a bitch of mine to any hound that I had not had in my own kennel where I could get to know him thoroughly by running him for at least several weeks! I was never anything but happy with that decision.

Well, after those first three matings took place, and the pups grew up, things got out of hand for a while. I could never even begin to fill the demand for beagles, and I went all out to produce as many good ones as I could in order to try my best to fill it. I had been selling many fox and coon hounds, but I soon realized that the beagles were more in demand. However, I continued to keep and breed both. Sometimes I would have between 70 and 80 mature beagles on my farm, and I began letting out bitches in whelp to farmers in the area. I would let them take as many bred bitches as they had time and space to handle. Then I would let them have any pups I didn't want after the litter was born, and I would pay them a nominal fee for the ones I took. Soon my number of beagles began to sore, and I owned more than 150 at one time on several occasions.

Feeding them all was, of course, a problem, but not like it is today. I had plenty of cows on the farm, and during the warm months I fed cornmeal mush mixed with skim milk. When the weather was sufficiently cold to keep meat from spoiling, I used to buy old horses. I would buy them for a small price and a neighbor boy would skin them out for the hide. Altogether the cost to me was trivial, and the hounds had plenty of fresh, raw meat.

In addition to this, they would many times catch their own meat. In an average day of running, the pack would kill several rabbits, and would eat them among themselves -- then go off to find another. If a rabbit made the mistake of getting into a brush pile, the pack would literally surround it and when a hound or two forced the rabbit to duck out by going in after him the rabbit suddenly found himself in a ticklish spot. Often as not he never had a chance to repent for his mistake. I often would kid the boys at the field trials later on by telling them that my hounds had to be good to survive, since if they couldn't catch rabbits they would likely starve to death! More than one of them, I'm afraid, took me too seriously, but it was a lot of fun at that.

I kept my fox and coon hounds tied, or in sheds, but the beagles were allowed to run whenever they wished during the day, or at night if the big hounds were not loose.

It was not until later on that I attended field trials, and at that I never went to an awful lot of them. For about six years I attended several each year, and that was that. One year I was president of the Hawkeye Club, but I was never too keen about cottontail field trials, and I was too far from the hare trials. My hounds always managed to be awfully hard to beat at the trials, and I have no idea how many of them I sold that went on to finish their field champion-ships, I know I owned many of them that could and would have earned their titles if they had been campaigned. Many of my best hounds I kept for breeding purposes so that they never got to trials; though they were severely tested before becoming brood bitches or studs; and other good hounds just weren't good enough to compete against others I owned. Many of the hounds I sold in all parts of the country went out and won trials, and I found after I began to attend trials that it was often difficult to find good competition for my best hounds. Now and then a real hound would up and give some of mine a licking fair and square, but it didn't happen very often. In general terms, if I went to a trial with a string of hounds, and they managed to overcome the hazards and brakes at first series, they generally picked up the chips at the end.

Once my stock began to enlarge, I sold many hundreds of beagles before I had an opportunity to look them over and decided just how good they actually were. One thing that stood out was that virtually every litter I bred and raised were good ones in the field, and many of them were good in the shows at that time, though they wouldn't stand a chance today in shows. In my entire breeding experience over more than 20 years, and involving many hundreds of beagles, I only ever bred three hounds that were so poor in the field that I didn't feel justified in selling them to field trial men, or for gun dogs. Actually, I had an excellent start with quality, and I did my best never to let that quality lag, once it got started.

I owned, bred, raised and trained so many hounds that it would be impossible for me to elaborate on even most of them. Some stand out in my mind clearly to this day as being the very best quality Champion Yellow Creek Sport is of course one that stands out about the highest. It is odd that he should have been a show champion, when today he would not have stood a chance on the bench, and that he should have been left without the title field champion, when today he would have been just as unbeatable; once he managed to get into second series, as he ever was.

Yellow Creek Sport probably figures in more pedigrees of the nation's best hounds today than any other single hound, and he was by no means an accident. From Muskeag Sportsman, I elected to carry on my Yellow Creeks through Yellow Creek Bob. It is interesting that Sportsman, Bob, and then Sport all had the same voice, incidentally. From Bob came Yellow Creek Sport, when Bob was mated to Fd. Ch. Yellow Creek Jessica. I don't want to get into breeding until later, but Yellow Creek Jessica almost couldn't help producing good stock when bred to Bob, as she was one smart hound, as well as being extremely capable in the field. When she was about a year old she whelped her first litter of puppies, of which Sport was one. At weaning time they were all placed in a sort of corral made of boards, and about eight feet high. Jessica would go out and still-hunt rabbits so they would not hear her, and she would catch them, or, if running in a pack when the pack caught a rabbit, she would wade in and get whatever remained if she had to fight the entire pack. Then she would bring the rabbit back and deliver it to her youngsters, over an eight-foot board fence!

My daughter came running into the house one day and told me that she had seen Jessica jump up to the top of the fence with a rabbit in her mouth and drop it to the puppies. I found it difficult to believe, but went out to investigate, and after a short time, in came Jessica toting a rabbit in her mouth. She sort of measured off the distance, got a good start, hit the boards on a certain part of the fence where she could get the slightest toe-hold, took one more leap from there and dropped the rabbit deftly over the top. No corral without a covered top would hold Jessica for long. In the field she was a real worker, true to voice, fast, and brains to let. Yet when a rabbit was caught, if she had puppies, she grabbed it and made a beeline for the pen.

Knowing both Yellow Creek Bob and Jessica as I did, I knew they should have exceptional offsprings, and sure enough Sport was about the best built and best running beagle I ever owned. He later became my yardstick when it came to whether or not a hound was well built. He finished his show championship in straight shows. When he was a derby I took him, his dam Jessica, and his granddam, Ch. Martin's Ada, to the State Fair and dog show at Sedalia, Missouri. Jessica was placed over Ada, her dam. Sport won his class. Later I sent four that a judge selected for me on a Southwest circuit of shows. The four, Yellow Creek Sport, Yellow Creek Jessica, Yellow Creek Bessie, and Yellow Creek Keith were handled by Gene Moses, a Joplin, MO, reporter. Sport won his championship easily, and the rest did well. Jessica, if campaigned extensively, could have finished and easily been a dual champion. Later the next year I took her dam, Ch. Martin's Ada to the St. Louis trials where I sold her to Ike Carrel, and her little sister, Yellow Creek Bessie, to Walter Leck.

Sport was left with my friend Gene Moses for a year or more as he was very much attached to him. He took Sport with him in his car wherever he went, and Sport enjoyed his companionship immensely. He was obedient at all times, and would ride like a sardine packed in a crate of other dogs with never a cross expression. He would always emerge with a friendly wag of his tail, and was a friend of everyone.

Sport never finished his field championship because of the way I felt about field trials. I gave him four trials, and he won two firsts and a third. In the one trial in which he was not placed, he had a tiny rabbit, and while he handled it well, the judge felt that he did not have opportunity enough on such a rabbit to compare him favorably with other hounds that had better runs. When he placed third he beat both of his first two bracemates handily. The third bracemate paused during the run to lay in some water, while Sport was picked up running. Sport was brought back again to run, and I figured it was for first place. Instead when the run was over, the hound that had quit to lay in the pool was given first place! That was the last beagle field trial in which I ever entered a hound, so Sport never had a chance after that.

His style of running was grand to see. He did not appear to be a fast dog, but in a pack he was in the lead most of the time. With a bracemate, he always seemed to be just a jump ahead, and at the checks, doubles and tangles his brains and keen nose were the key to many that seemed impossible to solve. He was one of the few hounds I ever saw that almost never lost his rabbit. He could run a rabbit no matter how hot or how cold the weather might be, and his nose was about the best I ever saw on a hound. He would cold-trail often, but never give tongue until the line was hot and the game moving.

If I were going to pick out a possible flaw with Sport, it was that he was not a first class (tree) barker, at a hollow log, or hole in the ground. He would tree at brush piles alright. I have been in sight of a rabbit entering a tree or log and watch Sport approach the tree, sniff it over carefully, circle it a few times and look around every way to see if he could see me coming. For a short while he would sniff around, then take off to find another rabbit. In other ways I would not want him changed at all.

Yellow Creek Sport had this kind of sense. One time Hounds & Hunting magazine published a highly controversial article on whether or not a hound can reason. Shortly afterward, I was at Hawkeye trial and had tied up Sport and Yellow Creek Bill in the same kennel. I had them tied to leads from opposite corners of the pen in such a way that they could only get their heads together up to about their eyes--this way they could not get tangled. I placed a pan of dog food between the two hounds, and they went at it. Bill was the kind of hound that gulped his food, and would eat his own weight if permitted to do so. He started eating hastily while Sport ate in his accustomed slow, careful way. Soon it became apparent to Sport that Bill was going to eat more than his share, so while I watched he picked up the pan of food with his teeth and deliberately set it down where Bill could not get any of it. Then he continued to eat in his own careful fashion. I repeated this experiment several times in the presence of other beaglers.

I've always insisted that a hound be a good "sticker". I want him to stay with those checks until they are solved, or there is no answer to them possible. I don't know just how long Sport would stay and run if you and the dogs would stick with him, but I have run him hard six days a week regularly, and then turned it on even more on Sunday. The longest continual running I ever knew him to take, part in was in March of one spring. I had about 35 grown beagles around the place of such quality as Yellow Creek May, the old Warhorse Wheatley's Chieftan, Yellow Creek Ed, Yellow Creek Daisy, etc. They were running at six am that particular morning in hilly country covered with timber and pastures -- the sort of places rabbits love to run in. With the help of my boys, I was milking 14 cows and mending fence in between times, and the pack ran all day within hearing distance, and sounded fine. When I quit making fence to do the chores and milk and feed the dogs, quite a few hounds had come in. I got the dogs food ready and gave them a blast on the horn, and brought all the rest in but six, and Sport was one of them. Since these six hounds knew it was time to eat, and since they must have heard my horn as they always did, I could only conclude that they would rather stay in that run than eat!

After I ate supper, I went out and blew the horn some more, with the result that two more hounds came in, leaving Yellow Creek Daisy, Yellow Creek Wahoo Sam, Yellow Creek Jonas, and Yellow Creek Sport. They were all still going strong by all indications, and I just said to myself, "Go to it," and went inside and went to reading Hounds & Hunting, which had come that day. By eleven o'clock, I had read about all of it, and I stepped outdoors for a moment to find out what was doing. Sport was as strong in voice as ever; Daisy was barking every now and then, but showing signs of tiring; Wahoo Sam was behind, but still trying. I came in and went to bed wondering to myself if the great field champions I had been reading about all evening could be any better than Sport.

Sometime later in the night, Sport's full-tongued cry woke me up. The house was situated on a hill, on each side of which were streams, one of which was a branch of Yellow Creek. The yard was surrounded with fence, and the beagles had opened holes on two opposite sides through which they came and went regularly. The rabbit had cut across the yard and Sport was staying right with him. He was running alone to the best of my knowledge, though I didn't stay awake long enough to see if there were any other hounds behind him. If there were, they were well out of the race. As I dropped off to sleep again I was thinking what a real stayer he was.

Next morning I ate and went out to milk the cows and I could hear another race on. Some of the hounds that had come in the evening previous were out running a rabbit. About the time I finished milking I spied Sport emerging wearily from his sleeping quarters, and presently he pricked up his ears, then lit out after the pack. Soon he opened in the race, and at first his voice was very course and husky, but soon it cleared and was as clear as ever. I quit work around four that afternoon and went out and caught Sport and brought him in to feed him. I am satisfied that he had not more than five hours rest in the previous 24 hours running. I never owned or saw another hound that had that kind of sticking quality.

One time at a Hawkeye field trial my brother and I had several of my Yellow Creeks out running in pack and some bystanders had accompanied us. After we had watched a while we all walked back towards the kennel and someone asked if it would be all right to leave Sport and the rest running. My brother replied that it was safe, that Sport would certainly come in when he was finished, as would the rest. I agreed with brother's idea, but was not at all certain as to when Sport would decide he had enough. I decided to set out and pick up the hounds. Jack Croy, who was among us, came along with me, and after running about a mile we headed off the hounds. Sport was leading in his usual way, and we managed to get all the hounds on lead. As we were hiking back along an old road, Jack noticed that Sport was limping and he said, "That hound is lame." Reaching down he picked up a forefoot and discovered a thorn in the ball of Sport's foot. It was driven right straight in, perhaps a half-inch, and the end was all frazzled where Sport had been wearing on it. In spite of the thorn in his foot, Sport had been running several hours on it, and had been beating the pack as well.

When W.E. Wakeman, of St. Joseph, MO., came over to breed a bitch to Sport one time it was during the hot dry spell of August. After the service, about sundown, W.E. decided to stay over and breed the bitch again for better insurance. We talked dogs until bedtime, and then retired. When the roosters awakened us at daylight, Sport had a bunch of hounds upcreek about a mile running. I told Wakeman they would be in when it got hot, which would be soon, but it didn't happen that way. We had dinner at noon, and since I was scheduled to pitch a ball game in town that evening at three p.m. and Wakeman had 120 miles to drive back home, we left at 1 p.m. while the mercury hung at 105 degrees in the shade. Later I learned that the pack came in about 2 p.m.

The day Ed Ponzi came to buy Sport, it was 110 degrees outside. We went out to run dogs and Ponzi will testify that those hounds ran and ran and ran some more, heat or no heat.

Knowing all this, is it any wonder that such great running and producing hounds as Sutton's Sport, Sammy R, Gray's Linesman, Yellow Creek Ben, and other "greats" too numerous to mention, should come from him, directly or indirectly?

Yellow Creek Bobbie was another hound that had all it took. He was from Yellow Creek Daisy from a mating to Yellow Creek Bob, and was a real hound. He was nearly the hound Yellow Creek Sport was, but not quite when it came to all-round considerations. I kept only him from his litter after they were all trained, and sold the rest. He was too good to part with. Bobbie was outstanding right from the start, and had the truest hound voice I every heard. I was handicapped by having Bobbie when I did, since he was by my standard too closely bred to most of my bitches to be used on them as a stud. I kept him for awhile and entered him in some field trials with excellent results, but later I reluctantly sold him, since I could not get good use of him for the foregoing reasons. His name appears in many pedigrees of fine hounds today.

It would serve no purpose to dwell too long on Bobbie, and the way he ran in training and later at field trials, but one incident bears relating. At the Hawkeye field trial held at Dawson, Iowa, in 1924, Bobbie was braced with Shady Shores Shortbay. They had been down for some minutes, and I, as Bobbie's handler, was running just behind judge Fabian Laraunt a few steps. The rabbit elected to run up a steep, thickly-covered hillside, which terminated abruptly in a cliff some 40 to 60 feet in height, which overlooked a river. Along the very edge of the precipice was a cloak of dense bushes, and the rabbit, knowing well the country, headed straight for the cliff. At the last instant, a few inches from the sheer drop, he cut left along the cliff, and scampered away into some thick cover. Over the hill went the two hounds, Bobbie in the lead, into unknown perils. By the time Bobbie saw the river he was right out over it, and falling. Contrary to reports from some others, nobody saw this fall except judge Fabian Laraunt, who threw himself on his stomach in time to see Bobbie bounce off a large, mud-covered rock and fall into the river. I was only a few strides behind, yet by the time I could throw myself on my belly and peer out over the edge, Bobbie was swimming across to the other side of the river. I shouted to him and he heard me and began to strike out directly upstream into the current. After what seemed like hours to me he finally found a place he could get ashore, and I ran down to see how badly he was hurt. But I never found him. He scrambled up the bank through thick weeds, made his way back to where Shortboy was working a check near the place where the accident had happened, and away they went. He went on to win the trial in spite of being in pretty bad shape along the left front shoulder, and was the talk of the field trial season that year I can tell you. I was some proud of Bobbie that day, as I was on many other occasions.

    This was the kind of hound I always tried to develop and carry on, the kind that don't know quit as long as they have a breath of air and an ounce of energy in their bodies.

    These traits I have mentioned briefly as yet, but they are of the utmost importance. This is especially true when deciding which hounds to breed. I always bred top quality to top quality for these traits, and after while I found I had it in most of my litters. And that too, is getting ahead of the story.

Martin's Ada was another great hound that came to Yellow Creek. I did not breed to her, I got her in a trade from Fred Martin, Wilmington, Del., with whom I did a lot of business. In those days show hounds were built for looks that were based on field performance ability rather than for looking pretty, and Ada wasn't stiff at all. She was an excellent bitch, and after I had time to look her over and appraise her fully I liked her a great deal. Bred to Martin's Sapper, she produced Yellow Creek Jessica. Later on I sold Ada to Ike Carrel.

Seminole Ben was another good hound I got from George A. Flammer, of Roseland, N.Y. He was fleet of foot, and fit into my breeding pattern just right. Yellow Creek Sport, when bred to one of Seminole Ben's bitches, Yellow Creek Sparky, produced Yellow Creek Ben. Seminole Ben's idea of work was speed. He ran a good rabbit, fast as lightning and energetic in working out his checks. He aimed to get that rabbit run in a hurry, and did it clean. He was one of the best starters I ever saw, and all of his offspring were good in that department.

I had Ruffner's Lefty here for a while, and he was a nice little hound. He was not outstanding, to my idea, but he was completely honest in his work, though slow. Many hunters like slow, steady-going hounds, for a variety of reasons, and I sold most of Lefty's offspring to those who liked that kind of hound and he turned out many for that purpose.

Beaglers have many times asked me to name the hound I thought was the best of all the Yellow Creeks, and of course that is unfortunately an impossible thing to do since they were scattered over more than 20 years. It is not possible to more than speculate what a hound might do if run against another one, and since many of mine never ran against others due to having lived out their prime, or their entire lives, before each other, I have no way of comparing them as individuals. I don't believe a hound ever lived that was better than Yellow Creek Sport in his prime, and yet sometimes I wonder about Yellow Creek Bob, Yellow Creek Bobbie, Muskeag Sportsman, and.... there are too many to compare. I had many excellent bitches, and some of them might have walked away with the prize! I believe, though, that for all purposes, Yellow Creek Sport was the best hound. But, I could be wrong.

Whenever I went to the field trials with a string of hounds, I knew I would come away with some ribbons, or that something was wrong with the trial. Sometimes I did not get real competition, which while it sounds like boasting, is nothing of the sort. There were some good hounds around in those days, but it took superior ones to compete seriously with my Yellow Creeks.

One year when the Hawkeye field trials was being discussed and planned, some difficulty developed as to where it should be held. One member wanted to see the trial held near his home town of Davenport, Iowa and was quite strong in his feelings about this. However, the club over-ruled his suggestion, and decided to hold it at Dawson, Iowa. I was attending the Sangamon, ILL., trial with Harry Lewis the weekend previous to the Hawkeye date, and word got around that the irate club member had written to other members of the Hawkeye club saying he and a few others were not going to enter their hounds at the Hawkeye in protest at its being held at Dawson, and that there would not be enough hounds for licensed points, according to an old regulation in use at that time. I wired to my boy at the farm to "pick up any ten hounds" and ship them to me at Dawson, Iowa immediately, which he did. When we got there the next weekend, however, there were more than 60 hounds there already. I only ran half of my hounds therefore, and won 1st in the 15" derby, 2nd the all-age, 15" class, 1st and 2nd in the all-age 13" bitches, and some other places I do not at this time recall. So, the Yellow Creeks were up in there by any standard, and I could take most any of them to a trial and not worry too much about getting at least some recognition in spite of the inadequacy of field trial testing.

There is a list a mile long of hounds I recall just offhand that were good ones. I could not say how many field champions, or field champion quality, but many of them. I sold beagles into the thousands, all over the United States and most of the time, up until the depression days, could never fulfill the demand.

My most effective years were from about 1909-1929. When the depression struck, things got very bad here in northern Missouri. When it got so bad that I took a dozen eggs to the store for the 2 cents per dozen we had been getting, and the buyer said he couldn't even pay that any more, I gave up. I hadn't sold a hound in weeks, and could no longer afford to keep them. I gave them all away but two or three, and when W.R. Watson of Bristol, Virginia offered me $350 for Yellow Creek Kennel name, along with 2 or 3 of my hounds, I gave it some thought and finally accepted. I needed that $350 badly. Later, the name was sold to its present owner.

It took me quite a few years of hard work to make a financial comeback, and while I have raised a few hounds since the depression, I've never gotten back into it to any large extent. In recent months my health has been poor, which was due to bad teeth and is to be expected when you reach 67 years. But, when I get back on my feet I expect to raise some more beagles.

Money is a problem of a breeder of beagles, let me tell you. The price of good ones is never high enough to cover all the bills, from food costs to sickness and loss of good hounds by their being stolen, poisoned, or dying from illness or accident.

The Yellow Creek hounds started many a kennel going that is today still in business, and turning out good hounds. I do not, of course, get around to see much of what is going on today, so I don't know what the quality of hounds is the country over. But I have noticed in the beagle magazines that most of the good ones go back in some way or other to some of the hounds I thought the most of.

There is a story behind Harvey Low and myself that might bear repeating. One time Harvey wrote to me asking about what I had for sale, and it just happened that at that time I was in need of some money. I went out and got the pack running and after an hour or so I picked out one hound that looked to be a good one. I watched his work closely for a while and went back to the house and wrote a letter to Harvey detailing in as exact terms as I could just how that hound ran a rabbit. I set a price of $150. In a few days I received a check for that amount with shipping instructions. During the next few years on twelve different occasions I sat down and wrote to him when I was a bit low on cash and in the same way I described a particular hound. Every one of those twelve times I received an immediate check from him for $150. One time when I did this he sent me a check for $650 with a note saying, "While you are crating that one, put in Yellow Creek Sport!" I sent him my own check for $500. Though it was not easy to do, it was easier than shipping Sport away!

One of the hounds I shipped to Harvey Low turned out to be Yellow Creek Ben, and I suppose everyone knows the story of how Harvey found him one day with his hind legs and tail nearly completely severed by a mowing machine. This accident occurred when he was yet a young dog, and the legs were grafted back in place and the bones splinted. The tail never was the same, and the legs were a severe handicap to him, but he went on to become a field champion and a sire of note.

Everyone who ever owned or watched a Yellow Creek hound run when I was breeding them knows what they were like. To those who never saw them it is not possible to describe them in a satisfactory way. Every breeder's idea of a good hound varys and every method he uses to reach his goal varys, and all in all a great deal is left to the individual's methods and thinking. The Yellow Creek record stands alone as yet as far as I can see. What the future will bring forward it is difficult to say.

WHEATLEY'S CHIEFTAN
and one of his pups

Chapter III

Hunting Quality

As I have said repeatedly, the first thing I look for in a hound is level-headedness. Often it is possible to pick from a litter of youngsters one or perhaps two that stand out when it comes to this all-important quality. Closely allied with intelligence in hounds, level-headedness spells the difference between a mediocre hound and one of top grade.

It always shows through a youngster's eyes when he is yet a puppy if one knows what to look for. When you speak to such a hound he will look at you with an interested expression that seems to indicate he is trying to understand what you are saying to him. Sometimes the easiest way to locate such a puppy in a litter is to eliminate from consideration one by one those that do foolish things, or that do not have a sober, understanding expression. Watching a litter of puppies, one often sees some that yip and bark foolishly, that behave erratically, or that indicate in little ways that they are inferior to others. I never bred such hounds when they turned up in spite of what they might do in the way of field work later on.

There are other ways in which hounds indicate the use of intelligence and level-headedness. For instance, I have never known a male hound that was overly interested in bitches that were not ready for breeding to be worth anything in producing. On the other hand, a male that will not pay any attention to a bitch nearing her heat should be sidestepped in a breeding program. Such hounds are not sensible, and will pass the poor traits on to their youngsters.

I begin early in deciding whether or not a litter of puppies has good common sense, and is sensible. As they grow up, I continue to watch and make certain my observations are in line all the way. Yellow Creek Bob, Yellow Creek Bobbie and Yellow Creek Sport stood out as puppies to me very clearly. They obviously were not common dogs, based on their demeanor about the yard, and in their pens as youngsters. Later on their use of good sense was necessary when it came to settling down and picking checks under pressure, or after a sight chase.

A hound must have plenty of courage if he is to be a good one in my book. He must have the desire to go out and hunt and hut and hunt, and the courage to back up every inch of it. I don't like a hound that will back down from a fight if the fight is foisted on it by another. On the other hand, I don't like a hound that starts fights. A hound that will not back down, no matter what the odds, is a real one if he has ability, and is worth more than a million of those that will cower down in fear. A hound that constantly wants to fight is like a person who wants to fight--all muscle and no brains to speak of.

I like a hound that is close, but not over-exacting to a point where speed is sacrificed. It is important that a hound stays in to do his work where a rabbit might be frozen tight and sitting hopefully, or where the hound will not be starting other game, but let us not make so much of this method idea that we sacrifice the job we set out to accomplish, and then lose perspective...let us see the entire forest, and not dwell at too much length on an individual tree or two. A rabbit runs ahead of hounds much like a fox. When fox hounds are right up close to a fox, he runs a larger, faster circle, and he is in trouble unless he does so. He does not dare, as a rule, to hop around from tree trunk to stump and so forth, trying to obliterate the trail with intricate hazards. Take a slow running pack sometime, and drop in a few good, fast hounds and watch the run change! The same is true of running rabbits, except in the case of young rabbits, or where rabbits are run in exceedingly thick cover. Many times a rabbit will hop around ahead of pottering hounds and make a fool of them. In my experience, pottering hounds lose far too many rabbits to suit me, since a smart rabbit will eventually wind up the trail until it cannot be unraveled, even by the sharpest nose, and when hounds are working over the same area cover too long, losses must ensue. I like to see hounds do their work clean, without any trace of pottering, always moving their line forward as swiftly as scenting conditions and their own nose will permit it to be moved.

Some hunters prefer slow hounds on the theory that a slow hound will make it possible to kill more rabbits. This generally is a fallacy, though if a hunter is a poor shot, who prefers a rabbit to come hopping slowly to the gun, it might work better to have a slow hound. In general, while a slowly-trailed rabbit will make a <u>shorter</u> circle, a swiftly driven rabbit will return to the gun in less time. Often those who prefer slow hounds have never owned a <u>good</u> fast one, and this may well be the case since there are many <u>fast</u> hounds, but not many <u>good, fast ones</u>. A clean, fast hound is definitely and obviously indicating more talent for his job than a slow moving one under the same running conditions. The goal is to bring the rabbit around in the shortest time with the least losses, and there can be no question but that the fast, clean hound excels in that department.

Style can be overdone to a great extent, and is overdone too much to suit me. Results are infinitely more valuable, and if field trials were properly held, results would have to be considered of prime importance. <u>A truly good hound will not lose rabbits very often</u>. He may have to commit an occasional breach of space - etiquette here and there when scenting conditions or lay-of-the-land justifies it; or, under perfect conditions, he may not; but in such cases where there are good reasons for a hound to get out and find where the rabbit went, he should be permitted to do so without any demerit whatsoever, provided he works out in a manner that is indicated, by conditions. Where scenting is obviously tough, a hound will have to get out and find the line before the scent is gone altogether. If he leaves a rabbit sitting near the end of the line, and then must come back afterward to jump him again, that is not nearly so bad as that he work too close and so exactingly that he lose the line entirely when the rabbit did not elect to sit in close to the check area! It is impossible for a judge of hounds which are running braced, to weigh all these situations, of course, and this is an important consideration more to the hound man who wants to develop good hounds than to any field trial judgment factor.

Yellow Creek Sport didn't lose a rabbit once a week and that is no exaggeration. Many of my best hounds rarely lost a rabbit, and that is one of the best indications I know that a hound is running all right. I cannot subscribe at all to any theory which permits a hound to lose game and still place at field trials, or to be considered a good hound, and especially that hound should not be bred into a line of good hounds that do not lose game. Losing game is a large subject. It involves not altogether style, but good running sense and rabbit sense, patience, good nose, and may factors that are subtle and not understood completely by anyone. Suffice it to say that no matter how perfectly your hounds appear to run rabbits, if they lose many of them there is something wrong. You can get that quality of losing game into a kennel or a strain of hounds the same way you can get back-tracking or other undesirable factors, and it is a mistake to breed a hound that loses very many of them. The chief essential of a rabbit hound, or any kind of hound, is to trail the game until it returns, and surprising as it may seem to some field trial judges, that quality can be found in hounds provided it is sought out and proven in the proper manner. It admittedly requires more time than just the few minutes provided for testing in today's field trials.

I consider a hound's voice as being most important. I definitely like a bawl voice, and I want it deep and strong as a hound's voice should be. I do not like a chop-mouthed hound because after looking over many hundreds of hounds with different voices I have found those that have the machine-gun chatter will bark off a line much more frequently than hounds with a good bawl voice. If a hound does not have sense enough to know how to handle his bawl voice without letting it work to his disadvantage, he is just another hound. I once had a foxhound that had a bawl-mouth that was long as it was excellent in quality. It was so long a note that from the time he opened until he stopped you could count to 13 at medium speed -- and he led the pack hour in and hour out. For every hound with a bawl voice that used his tongue improperly, you will find a dozen chop-mouthed hounds that will do likewise.

Hounds today tend to be much too mouthy, in my opinion. It is not difficult to state when a hound is using his mouth properly, or when he is using it the wrong way. <u>Scent should be the only trigger that sets off a hound's tongue</u>. There is no other reason for a hound to open up whatever. You will see many hounds that let go with a lot of talk while harking to a bracemate or packmates, when they have no scent whatever and are just plain over anxious and impatient. These hounds should be cut out in a hurry. I will not excuse a hound for tonguing when he does not actually have scent that he can smell for himself.

Worse than overtonguing is a hound without enough tongue. Some hounds just don't ever have much, and others learn to keep quiet from being overcompetitive. A hound that will not give his packmates the benefit of his work, yet capitalizes on theirs, is a good one to be eliminated from any competition.

In general, a pack of hounds that will go out to run rabbits and wheel them around in an "I don't mean maybe" manner without cheating each other are good ones. I once had five bitches at Johnny Wyatt's place at one time that were about the fastest five you ever saw. They were a mother, Yellow Creek Gyp, and four of her offspring, Yellow Creeks Molly, Cricket, Sparky and Sally. The cover in that area was white oak timber without too much dense brush, and those five hounds could outrun any group of its size I ever saw. When the pups were just a year old they killed many rabbits daily, and during the entire time they ran together they killed a fantastic number. It would be hard to beat those five hounds.

One quality I always insisted on breeding into my hounds is the desire to hunt. When it gets so a man has to wade through hip-high briars while his hounds wait around outside for him to jump the rabbit, that is too much! All of the sires I used had that quality, and especially did Seminole Ben, Yellow Creek Bob and Sport, and Muskeag Sportsman before them.

I always like to have hounds that will bark "tree" at a hole or den, whichever the case may be. This is easily obtained if you have one that will bark at a hole to teach the rest. Also it can be quite effectively bred into a strain of hounds, since many will bark tree without any training, once hounds that will do likewise have been introduced into a strain.

Hunting quality is what beagles were originally bred for, and any steps that tend to minimize the importance of these qualities, or to reduce them from consideration in breeding, will do a great deal of damage to the breed.

YELLOW CREEK Mme.
and
YELLOW CREEK BABBS

(Yellow Creek Bob x Yellow Creek Molly)

CHAPTER IV

Conformity

It is with some anxiety that I regard the fact that beagles have now become the most popular purebred dog in America. I have seen what has happened to other breeds when they became so popular that they began to be bred by many different people with many different aims. The cocker spaniel was so "watered-down" after it became the pet of millions of Americans that it went from what was previously not a bad little hunting dog to just another "pretty" nondescript breed of dogs.

Popular opinion can be fine, and then again it can be not so good. People who have no idea why beagles were designed as they are, and who then embark on the task of "tidying them up" to fit them for shows are doing a terrible disservice to bona-fide beaglers. The trend of show beagles in this country is quite the opposite from the trend in England, as near as I can determine from this none-too-effective vantage point. Years ago when you saw a photo of a pack of English hounds, chances are they were all built and colored alike. Whenever you see hounds all built and colored alike, you know automatically that the breeder is placing his fist interest in looks, and that running quality must have been sacrificed. Yet today, since World War II, the English hounds in pack do not look alike. And their bodily proportions are vastly improved -- they are, in fact, like our show hounds used to be, and our modern-day show hounds are like theirs used to be.

Show breeders today cannot comprehend why it is that beaglers who insist upon having hounds that run rabbits well will not go along with their ideas of conformity. It is quite a simple prognosis -- show hounds of today have been redrawn along lines which remove them from any qualification of being able to run game as beagles must be able to run it in competition, or even on all-day hunts.

Years ago a breeder of good quality hounds could occasionally breed into a show strain and sharpen up the looks of his hounds without hurting too much his running quality. Today it would be fatal error for a breeder to ever breed our modern idea of show stock into a strain of good quality running beagles. It could only result in an influence of poor blood that would take more than his lifetime of proper selective breeding to erase.

Today show breeders have either forgotten about; or worse yet, ignored; the requirements that a beagle must possess in order to be a top-notcher afield. Now, I will, willingly, grant that in view of the failure of field trials on cottontail rabbits to test stamina, show men have every right to assume that stamina is not so valuable a trait as it once was, but nevertheless there has been a decline in the physical capability standards in beagle show judging in this country. And it is serious. Either the beagle must be split completely into two fields; show and field; or show men must study out the requisites of physical conformation where running characteristics are concerned, and breed toward those requisites.

The trend for the past twenty years has been to make the beagle prettier. His front legs have been straightened out at the expense of his ability to run as he should, his chest has been broadened to an extent that has harmed his speed afoot; his feet have been rounded in a "cat foot" at the expense of his balance and his sure-footedness; his body has been shortened at the expense of the shortening his running power and his shoulders have been stiffened at the expense of robbing him of his best muscle leverage.

I want to point out right here and now that all the "heart" or "courage" in the world will not permit a hound with today's show-conformity to stay in a grueling race such as hounds must stage if they are good ones! Take two hounds with equal sense and ability in the field, one of which is built for show by today's standards, and there will not even be a race between them. There is not a show hound running today that I know of that could conceivably outlast Yellow Creek Sport for more than an hour or so before he would leave it in the dust -- yet Sport was, in his day, a show champion! The conclusions from this are undeniable. Show men can ruin beagles -- but only if those who want good hounds breed to them.

There is definitely such an entity as the well-built hound, and the characteristics can, should and must be imbued into a strain of hounds by careful breeding if beagles are to be maintained at their finest peak. But, these qualities must be of a nature to permit a hound to do the job for which he was originally intended. On page 47 is a photo of Yellow Creek Sport. He was built, by my standards, just exactly right in every respect to carry out the job he was capable of performing. And the record of his many all day, all night runs is evidence that his body was fully capable of carrying out that job.

One of the principal reasons why show men must be more concerned with the fact that their hounds are capable of running in the field, and are built for the job, lies in the nature of breeding. On one hand, the easiest things to breed into hounds is color, and the next easiest is general conformity -- both can be obtained in a generation or two, and within a few generations at the most.

Yellow Creek Sport

On the other hand, the most difficult qualities to breed into hounds are the maze of complex, subtle characteristics that go to make up a good hunting dog. A breeder should always place these "hard to get and harder to keep" qualities far above such a minor consideration as color, and rate conformity as that which will permit a hound to carry out his hunting functions efficiently. There is a line between the two kinds of breeders, but the weight is mostly on the side of field men, who must work with invisible qualities that are easily destroyed, and once lost require many generations to revive. Whereas, show color and conformity can be retained readily, by comparison.

After a breeder of good field hounds spends a lifetime getting his hounds just about as he wants them, it is quite ridiculous for a neophyte to come along and take some of these hounds so carefully developed and start prettying them up at the expense of losing all the valuable ground breeders have gained. Sometimes it is a trait of people with inferior intellects to alter things without first thoroughly taking time to understand what they are tampering with.

Show hounds are a good idea if they emphasize traits that add up to a real hunting hound's qualifications. In fact, they could play a valuable role in the development of better beagles, for if a hound is out of proportion, or out of balance, he cannot do his work right. But, prettyness is not, or should not, be consideration where it hinders working qualities.

Here is a case in point that illustrates what happens when hounds are stressed for show, and then placed in a competition where they must compete against hounds that are built to do the job. I believe most any show man would consider Croy's Superfine Tony to be an excellent quality show hound, even by today's show standards, and would be quick to point him out as being a "show hound that could really run a rabbit." This being granted, let us bring Tony into sharp focus by considering one of his field trial runs.

One year at Indianola, Iowa, which is near DesMoines, we held a field trial at a place then known as the Log Cabin Camp. I had some hounds at the trial and one of them, a derby known as Yellow Creek Bill II, was put down with Croy's Superfine Tony. Now, Tony looked for all the world like the pictures of stud dogs of show type you see advertised today in the beagle magazines. He had stiff, straight-as-a-ramrod front legs, and his feet were round, but this body was just a little less cobby than those of today's show stock, which was some help to him. In the field he was not a bad hound at all for style, provided you attach the statement that he performed as best he could considering his poor running gear.

The two hounds were down on fairly rolling ground with quite a lot of hazel brush here and there. Bill led the early stage of the run by from 10 to 20 feet on the average, and presently the rabbit led off into a ditch, the bottom of which was powder dry, and the sides quite steep. The ditch ran north and south, as I recall, and the sun was in it all day long, baking out the soil. The two hounds went into the ditch and drove the rabbit down it a ways, to where he left the ditch and went into an adjoining field. Bill took the rabbit out, and circled at least two full circles, while <u>Tony could not get out of the ditch</u>! Now, Tony wanted to run that rabbit in the worst way, and he did his best in consideration of what he had to work with for a body--but in the end it was Bill that ran the rabbit. While Tony looks mighty fine on a bench, he looked awfully foolish in that ditch, and it certainly was no credit to his breeders, who had placed a hound with a lot of talent inside a body that was not equipped to do the job!

At length, Bid Lancaster, who was judging that day, helped Tony out of the ditch so he could continue the race. Yellow Creek Bill II got 1st that day, and Tony got 3rd, as I recall. I don't believe Tony ever ran again. There was a case where Tony, with the right body, might have been a real hound in the field--but hampered as he was with stiff front legs and shoulders, he could not perform his intended function.

All of which brings us right down to the quick. If the present day show standard is not what it should be, then how should a hound be put together in order to best do his job? Here is my "Show standard," based primarily on looks that will perform, and evolved after many years of watching hounds that could and couldn't do the job right.

<u>Feet</u> should be solid, thick and about 1/3 longer than they are wide--definitely not a cat foot. A hound gets most of his power from his two center toes, and uses his side toes only to maintain his balance in turning, or when on uneven ground. When the side toes are set up forward, as in a round foot, they interfere with a hound's foot-nobility, and detract from his surefootedness. The foot should be well knuckled, stout, and have plenty of strength in order to withstand long runs. A hound should not go forward on his toes to brake himself, rather, he should settle back on the rear of his foot.

<u>Ankles</u> should be sufficiently heavy-boned to take plenty of strain, of good bone for the size of the dog. This can be overdone, but it isn't in hounds today. It has been

argued that a deer does not require such heavy-boned legs, yet is of comparatively long endurance. I believe that the quality of bone found in a deer's leg is better than that found in hounds. At any rate, my experience indicates that ankles should be a little on the heavy side in preference to the reverse.

<u>Elbow</u> joints should be set out a little from the body--just enough to be noticeable when you look at them. This keeps the legs free from the body, and prevents them from constantly bumping into the chest when the hound is in motion.

<u>The front shoulder</u> should run slightly forward from the elbow joint to the shoulder joint, and then should lay back about 45 degrees to the shoulder blade. This provides maximum V-shaped pull of muscles in the foreleg, and results in maximum locomotion for every bit of effort expended by the hound when in motion. Also, by not being straight and stiff, it provides a cushion on which the hound constantly lands, rather than dealing him a straight-legged jar each time he hits the ground. This is an especially vital consideration when hounds are running up and down hills, or on all-day hunts.

Hounds not properly built around the front shoulders will be stiffened early in the run, out of it completely before too long, and will be no good in the field for a matter of days. I have seen this too often to accept any other diagnosis. The front view of the leg should be about straight--out from the body just a little. I have often wondered if the short windedness of a rabbit is not in some measure due to the poor characteristic build of his forelegs about the chest.

<u>Chest</u> should be extremely deep (see Yellow Creek Sport, pg. 47) and run to a very narrow bottom, or "brisket", near the heart. A beagle with a broad, flat-fronted chest will tire long before one with a deep, narrow chest, and will not run nearly so so smoothly. Some breadth, of course, is necessary, but not out of proportion as in the case of today's show standards. Compare a duck breast with its wide front, and a chicken with its relatively narrow breast, and notice that the duck must waddle while

the chicken can run along at a good speed, considering it is on two legs. Which can get up more speed afoot, and hold it the longest? The narrower front, but deep chest, gives a hound leg room. Just back of the legs, the ribs should spring out to provide plenty of lung capacity. This keeps the hound free from lung restriction when running, and enables him to breathe with maximum efficiency.

Body should be the least bit long, but never cobby. There is no word I dislike hearing about beagles more than "cobby." A short-coupled hound may look nicer, but when in motion the longer body is a great asset. It provides ample space for the natural doubling-up that a hound must do in order to get speed, and it prevents his stomach from constantly invading his lung cavity. Again, this is vital for all-day runs.

The loin should be extra strong and noticeably arched just enough to provide easy running, but not enough to give a hump-back impression.

Hind-quarters should be strong and well-muscled. Stifles well let down and extended out just the slightest bit in order to let the legs pass up past the stomach when the hound is in motion without rubbing, or restricting his speed.

Hocks should be well let down; not too high up, not too long, nor yet too short; and should be distinct and solid--not straight up, but tilting back somewhat. I prefer one that looks too crooked than too straight, since the proper hock gives more power for longer duration. Straight hocks will go stiff quicker, especially if the hound is running up and down hills, and if too stiff a hound can't last and be at his best for more than a few hours.

Both front and hind legs taken together are vitally important, and they must be in balance. Many hounds winning today in field trials are not capable of running well longer than the few minutes they are put down to run in a trial, and that fact can be determined by anyone who knows hound structure. These hounds are built wrong and it is a crime to permit them to breed more like them. They cannot take an all day job of running, and often when they do take it, only their courage permits it, with the result that they are not good for the field for several days until their stiffness has left them. Anyone who really knows hounds can look at many that are now field champions and know that they are too poorly built to perform their proper task. They look pretty with straight legs, but they cannot be all-day beagles. If you take a straight-legged, round-footed hound and place one hand under his chest and the other under his tail end, and thrust him forward, he will fall flat on his face. And he will be severely handicapped when running in hilly country, or when competing against good hounds over a period of time.

<u>A long neck</u> on a hound is essential to enable him to get down to the ground easily when casting for scent under tough conditions, and it should be strong enough to hold up a good-sized head. A shorter neck may serve all right when a hound is going to run for 10 minutes, but if he is to be called upon to give his best for a matter of hours, the neck wants to be long enough to give him an easy motion when casting for scent, and strong enough not to tire.

<u>The head and muzzle</u> are of the utmost importance. The muzzle should be long, and the head definitely houndlike in appearance. The ears should be set not too high, but again, not too low, on the head. The nose should be plenty broad, with wide, open nostrils to draw in the scent well. I do not know why, but after seeing thousands of hounds of all kinds and descriptions I am convinced that the shape of the head is closely connected with good field quality. The best hounds I ever saw had large, houndy heads, with nice ears, heavy enough to keep them from being harmed easily, and with intelligent expressions, and expressive eyes. I cannot over-emphasize the importance of the head being large and houndy, and the eyes being alert, understanding and expressive.

Yes, there is such a thing as a well-built hound. But, heaven forbid, it has nothing whatever to do with his being pretty! A hound looks awfully pretty to me when he has a nice houndy, sensible head, and his body is built just right to carry out the functions for which he was intended. Man has bred the hound family to suit his purpose for hunting. If show breeders prefer not to follow the running requirements when breeding their hounds, then it behooves breeders who have an interest in beagles that are able to perform their job, to stay in their own backyard and let showmen develop their own new and separate strain of beagles, based on looks only.

Presently they may vary so far as to develop an entire new breed of dogs, and perhaps that will be best from all standpoints. No group of hound men have a right to insist that a breed they use for one purpose should not also be used for another purpose, if that is the way the trend goes. Cocker Spaniels were never enough of a hunting dog that their value for that purpose could not be expended; but beagles are. They should not be expended of their field qualities for any other purpose.

If you want hounds that can perform in the field hour in and hour out, you will not go far wrong to try the above specifications. The Yellow Creeks were founded on them, and let me tell you they could run rabbits.

A good nose, incidentally, is often the difference between real fine hounds and run of the mill hounds. A good nose plus the good use of sense, is an unbeatable combination. However, a hound with a good nose, but with poor sense, will be beaten every time by a hound with good sense and an average or poor nose. At any rate, a good nose is vitally important. A good nose, attached to a level-head, with a goodly measure of ability, and the body to carry these qualities and traits, will add up to a superior beagle.

YELLOW CREEK LUCKY

"A Typical Yellow Creek Puppy"

CHAPTER V

Training

My method of training hounds is nothing very secret, and not the least bit complicated, but when it comes to effectiveness in evaluating hounds from all the important standpoints, it cannot be beaten, nor in fact, tied.

All theories to the contrary, I trained all of my Yellow Creek hounds; foxhounds, coonhounds, and beagles; strictly in pack, and no other way. And further, I want to state unequivocally that there is no better way to train hounds if you are sincerely interested in breeding good ones. In this one respect, at least, training ties in with breeding, and there are probably others.

Let us understand at the outset that we must separate the case of those who own a single hound, or no more than a few, or who do not intend to breed any of their hounds, from the case of the man who intends to breed hounds. I am quite willing to admit that many a hound can be, and has been, spoiled, or at least hindered, from running its best style by tossing them into a wild pack as youngsters, and expecting them to compete on equal terms. Many hounds cannot take this kind of training, and a fellow with a hound or two would not be wise to do such a thing so long as he must compete his hounds in field trials in braces, or so long as he is interested in bringing out the very best in his hound and does not intend to breed hounds, or to have his hounds used by anyone for breeding purposes. But a breeder, who would carefully and painstakingly train a hound just right, using every device at hand to insure that the hound was given no opportunity to be spoiled whatever, and then perhaps later on even cover up that hound's bad points by clever handling, is committing an error he will long be sorry for, and others will pay the price of. And, he will not be a successful breeder for long.

A breeder must subject his hounds to every conceivable test he can think of in order to insure himself against breeding to inferior material. Principal among those tests in his entire training program, which must be set up to give an advantage to no candidate. To be blunt about it, a hound that can be spoiled by pack running is not as good as one that cannot be so spoiled, and I for one never bred, and never will breed, to a hound that could not be trained in pack right from the start. Such a hound does not have the necessary stuff to warrant breeding to, regardless of how much ability he may offer as a consequence of careful and scientific training.

When I kept from 50 to 75 hounds on my farm, they all ran in pack, and what is more, they learned in pack. They were given their freedom when they were a few months old, and the day they felt the urge to go off and hunt with the oldsters, they went off and got in the pack. Now you may think to yourself, "how many potential good ones he must have spoiled." And I would answer that it wasn't long before the quality of my stock rose to the point where there were not many of them that could be spoiled by pack running. The fact that there are many beagles today that can be spoiled by pack running is a testimony that they are not being adequately tested for quality in field trials. You would not spoil many Yellow Creek hounds by running them in pack, believe me. Some did not do as well as others, but not many were spoiled. Those that were inferior went to hunters who wanted hounds to gun over, but I never believed in pampering hounds. But then, I did not rely on field trials as being any kind of test for my hounds when it came to breeding them. I didn't then, and I wouldn't today.

To work a hound carefully, and campaign him long and cleverly; then set him up as a field champion stud is really removing that hound from eligibility as a stud as far as I am concerned. I would never breed to such a hound, because too many environmental factors have guided his hereditary direction. I always sought to place more emphasis on breeding and heredity, and thus increase to its maximum effectiveness the bred-in quality of my hounds. This necessitates the removal of all coddling of hounds in training.

Yellow Creek Bobby and Sport and all the rest of the best ones all came up that way. They got into pack when they felt they were old enough, and they earned their way to the top. They made those other hounds listen to them, and that is my idea of a real hound, and a hound that I want to breed to.

I want to make it clear that I am in no way in sympathy with bracing hounds. So far as I am concerned there is only one time or reason for bracing hounds, and that is when two fellows go hunting, or running hounds, and all they have are two hounds; or when one fellow goes out in the field and he has a nice pair he likes to run. Otherwise the best qualities of hounds are being wasted when they are run--especially when they are competed--in braces.

When I had bitches farmed out with neighboring farmers, and I went to look them over, do you think I would pick out the ones I wanted to keep by spending all week bracing them? Of course not. They had been running together for weeks--anywhere from a few to 15 of them, of somewhat varying ages, and by the time I got around to look them over they knew full well what they could expect from each other. Why should I spend a lot of unnecessary time bracing them off and watching each one when I could put them down in pack and within a few hours at the most they would tell me all they had learned about rabbit hunting to date, and what is equally important, in pack they would tell me what I wanted to know about each other from what they had learned! A man who cannot take a pack of strange hounds into the field and look them over and understand that those hounds not only will tell him what they know about houndwork, but also what the <u>others</u> know, should study hounds some more before he sets out to do any breeding whatever. But braced, hounds will tell you only what they know about themselves and

<u>one partner</u>. That falls far short of the goals breeders set their sights by.

Now, there is one assumption I am making, and that is that the pack of hounds a breeder has are pretty good ones. To place a youngster in a pack of wild, cheating hounds will not be a wise move, for they will be forced to find ways to compete with these cheaters, and they may at length form habits that are undesirable, and at no fault of their own. Some will learn to go off and leave cheaters and find another rabbit, but that may introduce another undesirable trait into a strain in time. I believe it is wise not to have hounds in a pack that are too faulty--but then, a breeder of good hounds will not have that kind around anyway.

Training is just that simple. Let them run as often and as long as they wish, and pick out the ones that can take it, and can make the others look bad, and you will be well on your way to creating a fine strain of hounds.

CHAPTER VI

Field Trials

Ever since I was first connected with hounds in any way I have loved the thrill of the competition of a pack of good ones thrilling to the chase. Fox and coon hunts by the hundred could never dim my interest, nor satisfy my hunger for the thrill of the chase. Pack hunts as they are today, in the field and in the field trials, are fine. They may lack a bit here and there, but they do all the hunters want, and they bring out sharply the qualities of the hounds that are desirable. It took beagle field trials, on cottontails, to dampen my spirits, choke off my competitive urges, and finally force me to drop out of beagle field trials altogether before I lost all my friends.

I was endowed with the kind of personality that will not rest so long as injustice is being done, and there is so little justice about cottontail field trials that they have long since failed to interest me. To this day I will go a long way to watch a pack of hounds chase anything, but frankly I would not walk across the road to see a cottontail field trial, and I would never enter another hound in one. It has none of the spectator interest of pack running, provides no thrills for those who love to hear hounds run in pack, and if you win first place you have nothing whatever to be proud of when it comes to any indication that your hound was either the best hound in the trial, or that he is, in fact, even a top-calibre hound.

If these are strong words, then they represent a lot of careful study of all kinds of hound work, and equally strong conclusions as a result...conclusions I cannot muster up any amount of rationalization to remove no matter how hard I try. These field trials held with one beagle braced against another are in no way a satisfactory test of hound to my honest judgement.

Many beaglers of long standing and with keen minds have for years renounced the practice of bracing hounds in competition, and if beagling has gained more popularity for any reason other than that our population is expanding, then it has been at the expense of many good hound men who have departed from beagling in favor of foxhounds or coonhounds. With the country being broken up more and more in smaller plots, and foxhound and coonhound country being more and more invaded, beagling could be a fine solution for those who have spent a great deal of time with the big hounds, as well as for hunters who nowadays find it difficult to locate good hunting cover with plenty of game, and who find it satisfactory to run and compete hounds in the place of hunting to some extent. But, beagling must purge itself of its inadequacies.

It is inconsistent with good sense to try to brace off more than 10 hounds and run them in any way you care to do it for an entire day and know for sure when you finish that you have picked the best ones! Beagles are not trialed in their proper way when braced, since most of the fine qualities are left untested. It is foolish and illogical to assume that present-day cottontail field trials are satisfactory from the single stand point of testing hounds as they should be tested, and I don't think there is one single genuine hound man who can summon up anywhere near enough logic to support the contention that they are adequate for the task. I am not sure if there are any real beaglers who want to try. There may be a few who have had a few hounds for a few years; and never made much of a study of them, or a few handlers who find it better for their purposes the easy way, who will contend that cottontail field trials are all right as they stand, but that is to be expected.

With today's field trial classes, entries soaring in the hundreds, it is ridiculous to complete a field trial and have any notion whatsoever that the best hounds have been separated from the entries. King Solomon was supposed to have been one of the wisest men who ever lived, and if he had the eye of an eagle, and could fly silently over a field trial grounds today and watch every move of every brace, he still could not tell which hounds were the best in that trial, much less in what order they deserved to be placed! Only God alone could know which hounds were the best, and you wouldn't need any field trials at all if He would tell us.

Let us examine the field trial method just a trifle. It was never possible for me, when I had 50 to 80 hounds around that were all capable of winning field trials, to go out and pick out the ones I wanted to take with me to a trial in anywhere near the length of time that any brace of hounds is down in any cottontail trial today, and at that they were competing in pack for me, where energy requirements are far beyond that in the average brace running. Wouldn't I have looked silly going out and trying to determine which hounds to take with me to a trial by running off a "field trial" such as we see today!

To place hounds down in braces in routine order, with scenting conditions changing constantly, cover varying with every other brace or so, and judges looking at fresh hounds every brace--is it any wonder that hounds we see with field champion titles are just another hound when it comes to an all-day hunt? They are being trialed on their work for the first few minutes of their run, when in effect they should be trialed for a good part of an entire day, each and every hound on the same game, in the same cover, at the same time. This is no hastily drawn objection I have dreamed up over night, it is the way hounds have always been run, were designed to run and should run--in pack.

There is no area of the world where hounds of any kind are, or have ever been, run in any way but in pack, except in this country, and in this country the only people who run hounds of any kind, any way but in pack are beaglers, and among beaglers, only the cottontail men have elected to run hounds any way but in direct competition! If they feel lonely after looking at it this way, there is justifiable reason for it. There certainly is no sense to such running, by any logical standard. It is wise to be different when your position can be supported, but there is nothing more discouraging in civilization than to see people who are in the minority, and in it on a basis that cannot be supported logically.

When field trials originated, beaglers were competing from 8 to 10 hounds at the most, and had all day to do it in. Bracing bird dogs was popular at that time, and beagling followed errantly along. It might be conceivable to test hounds braced if you knew you were always going to have no more than a handful of entries; though it would not be the best way to my way of thinking; but beagling has long since outgrown that stage. When a little boy outgrows a pair of shoes, sensible parents don't force him to ruin his feet by trying to wear them anyway-- they get him some new ones. Beagling badly needs a new pair of shoes!

I have heard cottontail men say "look at all the wild hounds you see in a hare trial, and they run in pack!" And they cite that as a reason why cottontail hounds should be run braced; to prevent wildness. I know for a fact that some hare hounds should be run braced; to prevent wildness. I know for a fact that some hare hounds have been picked as winners of field trials that were so wild they weren't worth killing, but that is not testimony to the inadequacy of pack running, or of the hare trial system. It is the fault of judges who are inadequate for the job. A fault that has developed in hare trials in recent years is that judges incline too much to award points to hounds, whereas they should concentrate more on eliminating the faulty ones instead, at least until a pack has been narrowed down to a nucleus of all good hounds. For judges to concentrate on giving points to a hound that may have to be discarded when his faults are found out, and thereby allowing him to shield the work of good hounds by his faulty procedure, is not good judging. Yet, we are seeing more and more of it today. Hare trials can and should be an excellent method of judging hounds. Given judges who understand hounds from having spent a great deal of time analyzing them, and especially who have worked with good judges while learning; and the hare trial method is adequate for the job it is intended.

Not so with the cottontail trials, where the best judges on earth cannot make present methods operable with any degree of effectiveness whatever. There will always be poor beagles until cottontail field trial men make an intensive study of hounds, and then set out to establish an effective method of testing them. I can tell you right now that such a new method will not be adequate so long as it embraces the bracing of hounds.

I want to present here my own idea of an adequate field trial. It has been used by us poor Missouri farmers occasionally, when we wanted to see what we had from perhaps 30-40 hounds, and would work equally well with any numbers.

First, in installing any field trial system, we must set a goal. We must know what it is we are setting out to learn about hounds we are judging, and then we must devise a means of finding out these unknowns. Assuming that the purpose is in accordance with present American Kennel Club standards; that we are setting out to find a method of testing beagles in line with their intended hunting qualities as evaluated by The AKC; then we must set that as our goal. We are all closer agreed as to what constitutes a good hound than we realize, but for the moment will be content to leave the analysis to good judges, and merely design a system whereby good judges can pick the five best hounds from a given number, in order they deserve placing. Our system must be installed in such a way that we can accomplish our goal within the time of one day, and do it without fail at every trial regardless of the number of entries. It seems that this would be difficult, but actually it only seems difficult to the neophyte, inexperienced with hound qualities.

Now, for the sake of assuming a godly number of hounds, let us say that we turn out on a trial day and have 150 hounds which we must perform our test on adequately and completely. Disregarding the impossibility of doing so by today's methods, we will proceed on our own way.

We will start early in the morning by painting numbers on all the hounds while the judges are yet asleep, so they will have no idea what hounds they are looking at. As honest judges, they are in no way interested in the identification or derivation of any entered hound, except to refer to his work, and we will do our best to provide proper circumstances for such judges and judgment.

Now that the hounds are numbered; and incidentally measured at the same time in the event anyone should happen to take his dog to his car, and when removing him later for competition he should remove the wrong hound, and that hound be oversize or a hound of different quality; we can proceed.

The judges are summoned, and we start across the grounds. Upon reaching a spot suitable to the marshalls, we all cast our hounds and sit down to watch the melee. And such a melee will ensue as you have never before seen-- unless you are in the habit of watching a great number of hounds all try to run the first rabbit they jump, which fortunately I have many times. Now, it is safe to say that within 5 or 10 minutes we will find ourselves watching not one pack, but as many as 8 or 10, since many splits will follow, and some hounds will not care to pack, and in general it will seem like an awful mess to the new beaglers--much as if the novice were to watch a noted surgeon performing the early cutting stages of deep surgery, thinking it an awful mess--it isn't at all, as we will presently see. It is quite well ordered, considering what we have to work with, and the task we must perform. These hounds are in excellent condition, and their minds are sharp and keen. They have a lot of windsplitting to get done with before they are settled down to their work.

We will just take a seat beneath this pleasant tree for perhaps an hour, and not make any attempt to judge them. If we appear lazy, it is because it is such an excellent morning; the dew is on the ground and there are so many nice things to see, and the hounds are making that wonderful noise that thrills us all, and we should enjoy it for awhile before beginning the task.

Now that the hour is up, and the packs seem to be adjusted to each other, we shall proceed along with the judges to observe their procedure. Here comes a small pack now-- perhaps 15 hounds. There is the rabbit! He bounded across the field, and just this side of a thorn apple tree he cut to the left. We shall have an excellent opportunity here to see what sort of lead hounds we have. Here they come and...that lead hound overshot beyond the end of the line and gave tongue much too far. He pulled the pack with him, which is something we cannot tolerate. The judges are not ordering the marshall to pick up the hounds, number 78.

This is a small example of how our field trial will go. As the packs come past, the judges work into position for a marked line if possible; if not, they look over the work of the pack as it goes past; and whenever they see a hound commit an error of such gravity as wide swinging, cutting, skirting, improper use of tongue, etc., that hound is eliminated immediately. If the hounds should at any time lack for game, handlers will gather them up and hunt them, which will provide judges another opportunity to see what sort of searchers the hounds are.

By mid-day, the judges will have eliminated quite a number of the hounds, and the hounds will have eliminated many of themselves by quitting and coming out to their handlers. During this time the gallery is having an excellent view of the race, and everyone is enjoying himself listening to the music of the pack. There is not the usual boredom found at cottontail trials today, where everyone sits around waiting perhaps half a day to run his hound for ten minutes. There is not bitterness, as after each brace today, and complaints of "Aw, I got a poor break," or "my bracemate made a bobble, and I got the works for it!" All these hounds are down together, and if they commit blunders, or pull out of the race, there are no excuses...they just were inferior hounds.

By early afternoon, or before, we will have our running packs down to 3 or 4, with the number varying as rabbits hole up and the hounds harken to other packs.

When we have our hounds eliminated down to 15 or 20, we will then make an effort to keep them in one pack. This is not usually a difficult problem when the faulty hounds have been removed.

If they do not come together in one pack naturally, we will have handlers pick up the few that are in the smallest pack and place them back in the original pack. From this point on, errors will be most likely of a trivial nature. As we see each hound commit an error now, he is eliminated, and more and more we look to see the imperfections of style that set apart the inferior hounds from the good ones. Those that hang to the rear of the pack, and are beginning to tire to a point where they are no longer contenders are removed from pack as they indicate their weakness.

Eventually we begin to get down to the crucial moments of the trial, as the hounds are eliminated down to 6 or 8. Then the judge catches a bobble here, or a tired hound there, and out it comes and then another, and before we know it we are down to 5 hounds.

Now, in all this time we have not given a single "point" of credit to any hound. His points have been awarded silently by the fact that he is permitted to remain in the race.

These last five remaining hounds are our win and place hounds, and now begins the real battle. After these five run for a while, one of them is seen to be not quite so good as the others, and the judges agree that he should be eliminated. He is the Reserve hound. After while another becomes too tired to be a contender, and he is taken up, leaving us our top three hounds. Will anyone fail to visualize the dramatic moments as they tick off with those three hounds battling it out for first place?

Our judges are in no hurry, there being a matter of considerable time before darkness could call a halt to the race, and they want to be certain they find out which of these three hounds is the one they have been looking for. After while one hound has to give in, or he tires, or he shows in some way or ways, that the is not the hound the other two are, and he is removed, leaving us with the brace of hounds that are the two real hounds in that field trial above all others. We have at least come down to a brace of hounds, but we have arrived at the brace in such a way that we know beyond all doubts that it is the best brace of hounds in that field trial.

Everyone is on edge, and likely as not the owners of the two hounds are inside the clubhouse trying to avoid a heart attack as those two real hounds battle it out right down to the last ditch. In this battle there is no 5 minute, "second-series" run. The margin between these two hounds must nearly always be close, unless one is unusually superior. There is no quitting, no over-anxiousness, and no rush to get the brace up. They will receive every bit of time they need to demonstrate to the judges that they are the one hound in that trial that deserves to win. It will be no matter of a single check advantage, or a single drive, nor even two or three. When one of them is able to prove beyond a shadow of doubt that he is master of the situation, the other hound will be picked up, and winning hound will have that rabbit to himself where he can run it before the gallery until his owner sees fit to remove him! And there will be no doubt whatever in the minds of anyone on hands to whether the best hound won the trophy!

Now, beaglers, our field trial is over, and it's time to do some soul searching. What kind of a hound have you got out in the kennel, anyway? Have you got a hound that would be able to get into field trial such as I have outlined above, and stay in there with the best of them? Or is your hound a trifle this way, or a bit that way, and he couldn't stand pack work...or just what have you? It will be your inclination to regard my method coldly if you have inadequate hounds, I'll grant you; but if we search our conscience honestly and carefully, can we not state that we would like to own the kind of hounds thus trialed, and breed to hounds that could win such trials? We set out to choose the five best hounds in order of their quality, on one hand, and on the other hand, we accomplish this selfsame goal without any question whatever. What started out as a melee, ended up as a duel of the two best hounds at that trial, that day. The surgeon with whom we compared our trial, who began with such messy lot of cutting and complicated tying off of blood vessels; finishes his operation with the same clean dispatch.

Now, I believe that any real hound man would drive any distance to enter such a field trial if he had a real, top-notch hound. If he doesn't have a real hound, then how can he hope to win a field trial, and why should he even <u>want</u> to win one with a hound of common quality?

If a hound went out and won three such field trials, regardless of how long it took him to do it, would anyone doubt that that hound was a good one? It would give the back-yard breeder who has a few hounds a real opportunity to do some small-scale breeding. He could ship his good bitch off to a field champion stud and know beyond doubt that that field champion had what it took, and that is a vital bit of knowledge no breeder can count on today, and has not been able to count on for 30 years or more. When I was breeding hounds you couldn't count on a field champion stud, and field trials have gotten worse, not better.

Hounds are getting poorer today because of cottontail field trials, and they are going to continue to get weaker due to short runs in field trials. Then, being re-bred for style only in quality, they will further decline, and unless more breeders get outside the cottontail testing grounds to breed their hounds, beagles cannot survive what beaglers are doing to them and still retain good overall quality. Yes, we have some stock here and there yet today, but mostly because of a handful of breeders who test their own hounds their own ways, and because you cannot destroy good genetic structure completely in a few generations. Fortunately it takes longer than 20 or 30 years to upset a breed of dogs if any judgement at all goes into breeding. But, beaglers should realize that if they continue to breed weakness into their hounds, and to accept the verdicts being handed down in field trials today, they will one day find themselves getting only one good hound in every 10 to 20 litters, and finally none at all.

I could get at least half of most every litter that were real good hounds. It took me some generations of weeding out to get them just about the way I wanted them, but once up there, the strain remained steadily potent. Today breeders will tell you they are lucky to get one real hound in 5 or 6 litters; and I do not mean by field trial standards and attainments; and it is my belief and testimony that unless we rearrange our licensed field trials along lines that require hounds to run a good part of a day in pack to separate the weaklings from the good quality hounds, and subsequently begin to stress quality in all our stock the country over, we are going to breed the beagle right out of existence as a real hunting breed.

When it gets so you breed a litter of hounds and get none that will run a rabbit, you are getting there, and that is beginning to crop up more and more in our breeding programs. These poor quality hounds will go over from being the mere culls in a breeding, to being the dominant factors, and then many difficult generations of breeding will be required to bring back the quality we are swiftly losing today.

This is, and well should be, a stern challenge to beaglers the country over. If you have hounds with weakness--<u>if you know they cannot get out and run all day, and do it right, do not breed them</u>! You are miring beagling down another notch into depths from which it will be most difficult to salvage if you do. If field trial men will not look to see what is so obvious, then go to the trials for an outing along with the rest, and then afterward go home and test your hounds in packs, maybe along with some other fellow in the same boat. If you can get to some hare trials, get to them and see what you've got by those standards. Make sure the judges know enough to pull out the faulty hounds, and then test your own for stamina and keep testing them as long as they are in their prime, in order not to begin breeding a strain of sorry beagles.

Believe me, it is no accident that the Yellow Creek hounds had what it took. Yellow Creeks are still found in the pedigrees today because their genes are still popping out here and there and providing a taste of the hounds that came from a testing grounds that really put hounds to the acid test. But keep in mind that these old genes will one day run down unless they are revitalized by good, sensible breeding and testing of hounds. If bealgers permit this to happen it is of their own doing.

You bealgers may not like my field trial system at first--you may find a superior one, though in my lifetime of working with hounds I have never conceived a better one--but you must come around to face the fact that hounds must run in pack or you have only half-hounds, and you cannot breed successfully to half-hounds.

I have gone to great lengths to emphasize the folly of running field trials with hounds braced, and to install in its place a system of pack running because deep down I know that without that kind of running there never would or could have been any Yellow Creek hounds. I just wish I had a few of them back, to run them in pack for you today, and show you what a group of real hounds, all from the same kennel, can do. I think you might be quite surprised to find that they could run so smoothly in what some think are "wild, pack runs."

I am not an influential man today, and I can do nothing beyond this book to alter the course of events. But, if I had any means in my power to alter things in the field trial line, I would most certainly do it. Beagles are the greatest little sporting dogs that ever lived, and they deserve to be tested in accordance with their quality, not in accordance with a bunch of fellows who are not even fully acquainted with hound work, who want an excuse for an outing, with a party afterwards to celebrate a hollow victory, and who would rather have a nice day in the field than to enjoy the fullness of watching a real test of hounds and hound work.

When I was getting more and more disgusted with what I saw at field trials, and people I knew were getting disgusted with my disgust, I realized that many people would rather run a poor trial and have a happy day of it, calling those of us who could see the fallacy of trying to trial hounds under such conditions, poor sports, when we lost due to breaks that have no place in trials of any sort, than to take the trouble of getting better dogs and trialing them fairly. Before long I got out of field trials altogether. Too many times I saw hounds win and place that had no place even being considered beyond the slightest bit, and in many cases their owners knew it. And too many times I saw hounds get tossed out for something they didn't do, but a bracemate did, or for other equally foolish reasons. I couldn't join beaglers in favoring such trials, and I could not make beaglers see the wrong being done with them, so I merely withdrew and tested my hounds my own way. For years afterward I sold hounds of my breeding that today are in the background of many hounds, the best that are available today.

Only beaglers, through their clubs and eventually through the Beagle Advisory Committee can alter this course of events. If beaglers fail to make the alterations that are in order, beagles can only go downhill.

"YELLOW CREEK SPARKY"

(Seminole Ben x Yellow Creek Gyp)

CHAPTER VII

Breeding

I don't know what I can say about breeding that will help others who are already in it, or those just starting out. The subject is so complex, and so much is unknown to anyone, that about all I can do is make a few points known as they have occurred to me, based on my 30 or 40 years of breeding hounds of all kinds.

I will not attempt to evaluate the potency of any of the old time hounds I did not see, or did not see many of their offspring. Anyone who would attempt to carry out such an evaluation is just showing his ignorance of the facts of breeding. To evaluate hounds, and attempt to show that this one was more potent than that one, or carry more influence than another; unless the evaluator actually knew well and personally all the hounds involved; is really quite foolish to my way of thinking.

For instance, there are those who will contend that Alibi Billy was the greatest producer of any age, or that Afton's Uncle Sam was, or that some other hound was better than both. Many times these "experts" never saw any of the hounds involved. Actually, only the hounds that come within the experiences of a breeder can ever be evaluated--at least by present day standards and methods. And while there are those who tell us of the more scientific ways of understanding genes and chromosomes, and their makeup and possibilities and coefficients, there is sadly enough, nothing about my methods as yet that will provide us with any kind of satisfactory picture as to what hounds, or even bloodlines, are the best.

I saw many of the offsprings of Afton's Uncle Sam, and they struck me as being much like the offspring of Sheik of Shady Shores--hard going, but too mouthy. Uncle Sam's offspring never appealed to me a bit, and I never wanted any of his blood in my kennels. I saw some pretty good pups out of Alibi Billy, but they were inclined, if anything could be said to be characteristics of them; to be too slow afoot, and to lack the necessary drive. At the time these two hounds were being studded, it was popular to breed Uncle Sam pups to Alibi Billy, and vice versa. Uncle Sam was supposed to put the wallop in them, and Alibi Billy was to tone it down enough to make a good rabbit dog. I honestly cannot say how much effect actually attended this idea, but the cross did appear to make some headway from the standpoint of the records.

I saw a lot of the English hounds, and had a few good ones here at Yellow Creek. Wheatley's Chieftan was one of my good studs here for quite a while, and with one exception he ran an excellent rabbit. About one day out of 10 he would make every cast to the right regardless of where he knew good and well the rabbit went. It seemed to be a mania with him, and he never got over it. I never saw it in his pups, however, and it might have been completely environmental in nature.

I had Vernon Place Singer at Yellow Creek, and used him when I needed some substance in a bitch. He was not by any means an outstanding hound.

Fate often plays strange tricks on breeders, and can upset an entire era of hounds. At the time Alibi Billy and Uncle Sam were hot, the little hound I originally trained for Harry Stroh, Ganymede (Davey) Crockett, was around. And let me tell you, he was a real hound. I tried hard to buy him, but he was not for sale. I believe he might have given Uncle Sam an awful licking in the producing records from what I saw of his few puppies...but he died before he was three years old.

Just how to instruct a breeder in how to breed a fine strain of hounds presumes that the breeder has spent many years working with many, many hounds. He must watch them for hours on end, and study them from every possible standpoint. He must have time to run them, and study them, and keep them well, and mate them properly. And above all, he must have the insight that separates a breeder from the novice "puppy producer." When you hear a man say that it is all odds and luck in breeding good hounds, you know he is not a breeder. I admit, and even testify, that there is much luck involved as to just what results one will get in variations of quality, but a good breeder of any animal strain will gradually wipe out each fault in its turn, and eventually, if he has the talent for it, he will develop a strain of hounds that will run far above average in every litter.

I know of many breeders today who breed such a poor run of hounds that many of them will not hunt, many more have to be given away or destroyed, and only a few are real hounds. There are many reasons for this, which I will attempt to treat in a positive manner.

In the first place, it is necessary to realize that some hounds are good hounds, and some hounds are good hounds that will produce. There is a difference, and one that is vital.

For example, consider the three excellent males I obtained from my first mating of Muskeag Sportsman with Elora's Blue Peach...they were Blue Cap Revival, Elora's Blue Dispatch, and Yellow Creek Bob. You could take those hounds out and run them all day and I would defy any judge to say that one was better than the other in their field work, yet I selected Bob to carry on the line begun my Muskeag Sportsman. I chose him because he showed me that he had that something extra that would stamp his pups, and he had it. You find this quality by watching every aspect of a hound's demeanor, not only his field work. True, Revival and Dispatch are found in many excellent pedigrees but Bob is in 25 good ones for every one of them, and Bob was not used to the extent they were.

This brings us to a most vital and practical aspect of breeding, namely--the impression that the female line is stronger than the male line is a false impression in my opinion. My entire line of Yellow Creeks were founded and continued on the premise that the sires could in each generation stamp virtually the same quality on their litters as he had preceded them. Given the most potent male that ever lived, and the most potent bitch, and it is my contention that the litter will be at least 70 percent dominated by the sire; and if good matings follow, the line will carry on well. Good bitches are absolutely necessary to carry on the traits of the sires, and to reproduce the highest possible percentage of good hounds per litter. But the sire is the key to the overall quality. It might be accurately stated that the quality of the sires is borne forward through good bitches. In fact, a potent enough sire can even carry his quality through poor bitches; as is in the case of Gray's Linesman, Sammy R., etc. It has been argued that a good bitch produces more good puppies considering the number of puppies she has, then a popular sire of strong influence. This way of thinking does not consider that a popular stud is often bred to a mate of well-proven; or at least better proven; quality.

One time an Uncle Sam bitch, Atterbury's Little Floe, was bred to Yellow Creek Bob. I knew what the result would probably be, as I had seen many of Uncle Sam's get, but it turned out I was wrong. That litter was every last one like Yellow Creek Bob. While he was able to overthrow the influence of Uncle Sam completely off, Floe was a common hound, and I knew better than to try to keep and breed the offsprings.

I want to make it clear that I do not believe in close line breeding, or in inbreeding. The closest I ever bred two hounds was a dog to its own aunt, and though I had fairly good results, it is my opinion that any breeder who makes it a point to breed too close will breed himself out of good stock. I have seen it happen too many times to poultry and hogs to trust it in hounds. It may be just my farmerish idea, but I always kept as far away from line breeding as I could get, and I was never sorry for it. As long as the hounds being bred are from good stock, and they are good hounds themselves, there seems little need to intensify the strain by line breeding. An attempt to do so is to tread on dangerous ground. It may take longer to develop desired patterns of quality in a strain by staying away from line breeding and inbreeding, but it is safer and surer in my opinion.

Harvey Low and I believed alike, as near as I can tell, in every way when it came to training and handling hounds, but we disagreed in our breeding theories. He could never reproduce his strain after Wink of Shady Lake, which I felt was primarily due to his breeding too close, and possible to some extent to the introduction of too much pure show stock into his strain. For a while the Shady Lake hounds were excellent, but they failed to reproduce, and what good are hounds that will not reproduce?

One of the most important aspects of breeding is to understand that the level of potency can and should be raised with each generation of puppies. This is just another phase of selective breeding, I suppose, but one that is not considered enough today in my opinion. For instance, in weighing whether or not a hound like Yellow Creek Bob would do more to raise the level of potency of my hounds than to use, say, Elora's Blue Dispatch, on a good, unrelated bitch, I decided that since Bob had the slightest bit more overall quality to my eye than Dispatch, it was important that I use Bob. Breeding a lesser quality sire to even the best bitch is a mistake that will have bad repercussions. Each mating must be as good as it is possible to make with the hounds you have to work with.

For that reason it is vital to start out with the best bitches you can find, and also the best sire. Do not breed to any sire unless you know him personally, have seen him run in pack under plenty of pressure, and under all conditions. Then, if you know he is not a flash in the pan, and especially if his sire was a real one that had about the same quality as the youngster, it might be safe to breed to him. I always preferred to keep my own sire--then I knew what I was getting.

Here is a sort of a "picture window" into the operation of my Yellow Creek Kennels during one phase of my breeding program. At the time I had such quality bitches on hand as Yellow Creek Jessica, Yellow Creek Bessie, Yellow Creek Molly, Yellow Creek Mae, Yellow Creek Freda, Yellow Creek Lula, Yellow Creek Goldie, and a few more of that sort. I also maintained for sires, Yellow Creek Bob, Seminole Ben, Wheatley's Chieftan, Vernon

Place Singer, and a few others. Of course I had many other hounds, either striving for consideration, being trained, or beyond the useful age.

I used these hounds as follows: I bred Yellow Creek Bob the most, on all bitches that were my idea of just right for style, and with excellent results. Wheatley's Chieftan had an excellent voice and good bone and was a good searcher, so when I wanted to bring out these features in a bitch's litter because she lacked them a trifle, I would breed her to Chieftan. Seminole Ben was fast as greased lightning, did everything just right, and was an excellent hunter and searcher. When I had a bitch a little on the slow side, she went to Ben. Ben was a powerful influence, and I could see his characteristics in my hounds for 2 or 3 generations after he was finished as a sire. Singer ran pretty good, had plenty of substance, and his pups were usually good ones. When I had a bitch on the frail side, or too close to my other sires, she went to Singer for a litter to pick up a bit of bone. Within this framework of sires I had everything I needed to give that extra something to bitches I kept at that time. If they had any one characteristic in common it was that they were all <u>sensible</u>.

There were certain aspects that will bear a bit of enlarging upon, and one is the fact that I noticed after a few litters that Wheatley's Chieftan's bitches when bred to Yellow Creek Bob, if just right, or to Seminole Ben if a bit slow, were of excellent quality. I pushed this advantage as hard as possible, and for as long as I had Chieftan to work with.

Another factor is that my experience indicates that males can be used to better advantage than bitches in some ways. Bitches will carry forward the desired traits, but the males will keep in well defined terms the characteristics of the kind of hounds a breeder wishes to perpetuate. It is as if the quality within a strain were placed in essence in the sire or sires, and then carried over one notch, or one generation, by the bitches. Then, in its turn, the traits are invested in the sires, and again carried forward like a wave into the next generation by the bitches. This, as clearly as can be expressed, is the way my Yellow Creek strain was built. Probably the only drawback is that a man doesn't live long enough to get his hounds just exactly the way he would like them, and when he is finished there is no way he can train or appoint someone to carry on for him.

One of the little sidelights I have noticed in breeding is that a good-producing bitch with from 5 to 9 puppies will almost always have one female pup that looks, acts, and later reproduces, like its mother.

Also, if you breed an excellent bitch to a good producing sire, the offspring will average good, whereas the same bitch bred to a proper sire will carry out in that generation or next principal characteristics of the sire, and good quality will diminish.

Some characteristics, both good and poor, will seem to smoulder with a strain, and will pop out only occasionally. Yet, suddenly later on they may somehow come to life with considerable influence.

My experiences add up to this; my opinion of a hound with a 4-generation pedigree certifying that all ancestors within the 4 generations are field champions, is that it means less than nothing by today's standards. Give me time to go around and pick out from 3 to 5 good stud hounds with interlocking traits and 6 or 8 good field bitches with few if any field champions in their pedigree, and when I get through with 2 or 3 generations you can take the hounds that come from this strain and win any trial that is set up to pick out the best hounds, and in which the bolstered-pedigree hounds are entered! Any single good breeder can do likewise.

I believe the best decision I ever made in breeding hounds was when I bred Muskeag Sportsman rather than to either Afton's Uncle Sam or Rock City Sam. I believe the next most important one was never to breed to a stud I did not know well, inside and out. In those days more than today, perhaps it meant owning or running the study myself. The quality of hounds, both stud and bitch, should never be left to guesswork, or to mere field champion titles; at least for as long as field trials continue to be outings rather than hound-testing matches.

One of the worst things that can happen to you as a breeder is when you let your feelings for your hounds interfere with your judicious breeding of them. A breeder who "carries" hounds along is only fooling himself, and will never get far. When a hound has a fault, do not breed it, because you will only perpetuate it. If you are not honest with yourself and will not let yourself see faults, you had better buy hounds rather than try to breed them. Nature, a far wiser intelligence than that of mere man, has utilized selective breeding on a basis of survival of the fittest in developing all creatures. It worked for nature, and it will work for breeder; test your hounds thoroughly, breed them judiciously and with an open mind; breed only the best you have on hand, and then not too close, and you will slowly but surely establish a strain of the kind of hounds you like to see. That is the prospect for every breeder.

www.ingramcontent.com/pod-product-compliance
Lightning Source LLC
Chambersburg PA
CBHW021129080526
44587CB00012B/1201